THE 4 GOSPELS

Published by Collins Educational
An imprint of HarperCollinsPublishers Ltd
77-85 Fulham Palace Road
London
W6 8JB

First published 1998

ISBN 000 317673 8

British Library Cataloguing in Publication Data
A catalogue record for this book is available from the British Library.

Edited by Jo Ely
Cover and series design by Sally Boothroyd
Text page design by Sally Boothroyd
Illustrations by Belinda Evans, Bethan Matthews, Rhiannon Powell, and Julian Baker
Printed and bound in Great Britain by Martins the Printers

THE 4 GOSPELS

Teacher's Notes

Michael and Jan Keene

Collins Educational
An Imprint of Harper Collins*Publishers*

Contents

Unit Three: The miracles of Jesus — Page 90

Unit Four: The teachings of Jesus — Page 114

Unit Five: Further information — Page 148

Glossary — Page 157

Introduction

The Four Gospels

As a book, the Bible needs little, or no, introduction. It was the first book to be printed mechanically. The Gutenburg Bible, one of just 21 copies surviving from that original printing, was sold in auction 30 years ago for £1,265,000. Between the beginning of the 19th century and the present day over 3,000,000,000 copies of the Bible have been printed and distributed. Sales of over 10,000,000 a year worldwide are still recorded. Parts of the Bible have now been published in some 1,800 different languages and this number is increasing every year.

The most well known, and best-loved, translation of the Bible is the Authorised Version. This was published, at the instigation of King James 1, in 1611. It was the work of fifty scholars working in six groups. Until the 20th century, the dominance of this translation was unchallenged. But this century has seen the publication of a plethora of translations. The Revised Standard Version was published in 1952, followed by the New English Bible in 1970.

Four years earlier, the Roman Catholic Jerusalem Bible was published. The Good News Bible came out in its complete form in 1976 and since then further translations have followed thick and fast. They include the New International Version (1979); the Revised Authorised Version (1982); the Revised English Bible (1989) and the New Revised Standard Version (1989).

The Good News Bible has certainly been one of the most popular, and approachable, translations in recent years and this is the version used in the Junior Bible. But never before has the Good News Bible been published in such a child-friendly format. Additional material at the beginning and end has been written especially to appeal to young children and eye-catching and interesting photographs and maps have been added.

With any material of this nature, it is of vital importance to capture and sustain children's interest and enthusiasm. The four Gospels can be a focus of teaching for Junior RE as they cover the life, teachings and miracles of Jesus. Our focus on the four Gospels allows teachers to approach the life of Christ in the modern classroom.

The Teacher's Notes

The Teacher's Notes provide busy classroom teachers with easily accessible information about many passages in the Gospels. It suggests how to approach the passages and supplies copymasters to both encourage children to go back to the Gospels for themselves and to support them further in understanding key ideas and information.

The Teacher's Notes are a flexible resource which have been designed to support the needs of the non-specialist in the teaching of R.E., as well as to provide valuable professional development and ideas to the specialist R.E. teacher. The following are some key features of the Teacher's Notes:

- a series of factsheets to introduce and provide a historical background to the life of Jesus
- lesson plans arranged in topics from the Gospels, including the main events in the life of Jesus, the miracles and teachings
- supportive and accessible information on the meaning of passages from the Gospels
- summarised versions of key stories, for children
- suggestions for whole class and group discussion work
- copymasters to support, consolidate and extend each topic
- a comprehensive glossary of key words.

One of the advantages of the Gospels is that we have little idea of the order in which the events took place. Teachers cannot build up a biography or life-story of Jesus for their pupils. This leaves teachers free to follow any order which appeals to them rather than the order in one, or more, of the Gospels. The contents of the Teacher's Notes can, therefore, be used flexibly.

Why four Gospels?

After Jesus died, around AD 29, the Apostles began to preach about him throughout the Roman Empire. For a long time, little of their teaching was written down. The stories about Jesus and the parables told by Jesus were largely kept alive by word of mouth. As long as the original eye-witnesses to Jesus and his ministry were alive this presented no problems. They could pass on to the people just what they had seen and heard. Any questions about Jesus could be directly referred to, and answered by, them. Problems only began to arise when many of the original eye-witnesses had died.

Mark was the first to produce a written account of the life and teaching of Jesus, although he was not one of the disciples of Jesus. He relied heavily on the recollections of Peter, who was the leading spokesman for the disciples while Jesus was alive and also for the Early Church in the months following his death. Mark put pen to paper around AD 65. He was followed within a decade or so by Matthew and Luke. Luke, who was a companion of Paul on some of his missionary journeys, also wrote the Acts of the Apostles. Both Matthew and Luke made extensive use of Mark's Gospel when writing their own accounts, although they also had other documents or sources of information, long since lost, at their disposal as well. Because these three writers have so much material in common in their accounts they are called the Synoptic ('Seeing together') Gospels. A fourth account, John's Gospel, was written much later, around AD 95, and is very different to the other three accounts.

None of the Gospels present us with a full life of Jesus. And accounts of the same events have differences as well as similarities. There is a good reason for this. Each Gospel writer had his own reasons for writing. Matthew, for example, was mainly writing for Jewish readers, Luke for non-Jewish (Gentile) readers whilst John aimed his writing mainly at educated Greeks. At best, these provide us with a kind of snap-shot of Jesus, a picture seen through a lens which points in one direction and not another. Often what is left unsaid is as revealing and interesting as what is said.

Little wonder, then, that the Gospels are at the very heart of the Christian faith. They provide virtually the only information that we have about Jesus. Anyone who wants to understand why the Christian religion captivates the hearts and minds of some 1,500,000,000 believers throughout the world must begin by studying the Gospels.

FACTSHEET 1 The land of Palestine

Palestine, the land in which Jesus spent almost all of his life, was very small. From north to south (top to bottom) it was less than 170 miles long. The tip of the Dead Sea, at the bottom of the country, was only about 50 miles from the sea. In area, it was about the same size as the country of Wales is today.

The Jordan Valley ran straight down the middle of Palestine. To the north of this valley the mountains rose very steeply. The peaks of Mount Hermon, for example, were 3,000 feet above sea-level. The mountain remained snow-capped for most of the year. It could be seen by people walking along the streets of Jerusalem, many miles away.

The River Jordan rose in the foothills of Mount Hermon. It soon reached the Sea (or Lake) of Galilee. On its journey from there to the Dead Sea the river twisted sharply as it dropped rapidly downhill. The Dead Sea itself was some 1,200 feet below sea-level. This is the lowest point above ground anywhere in the world.

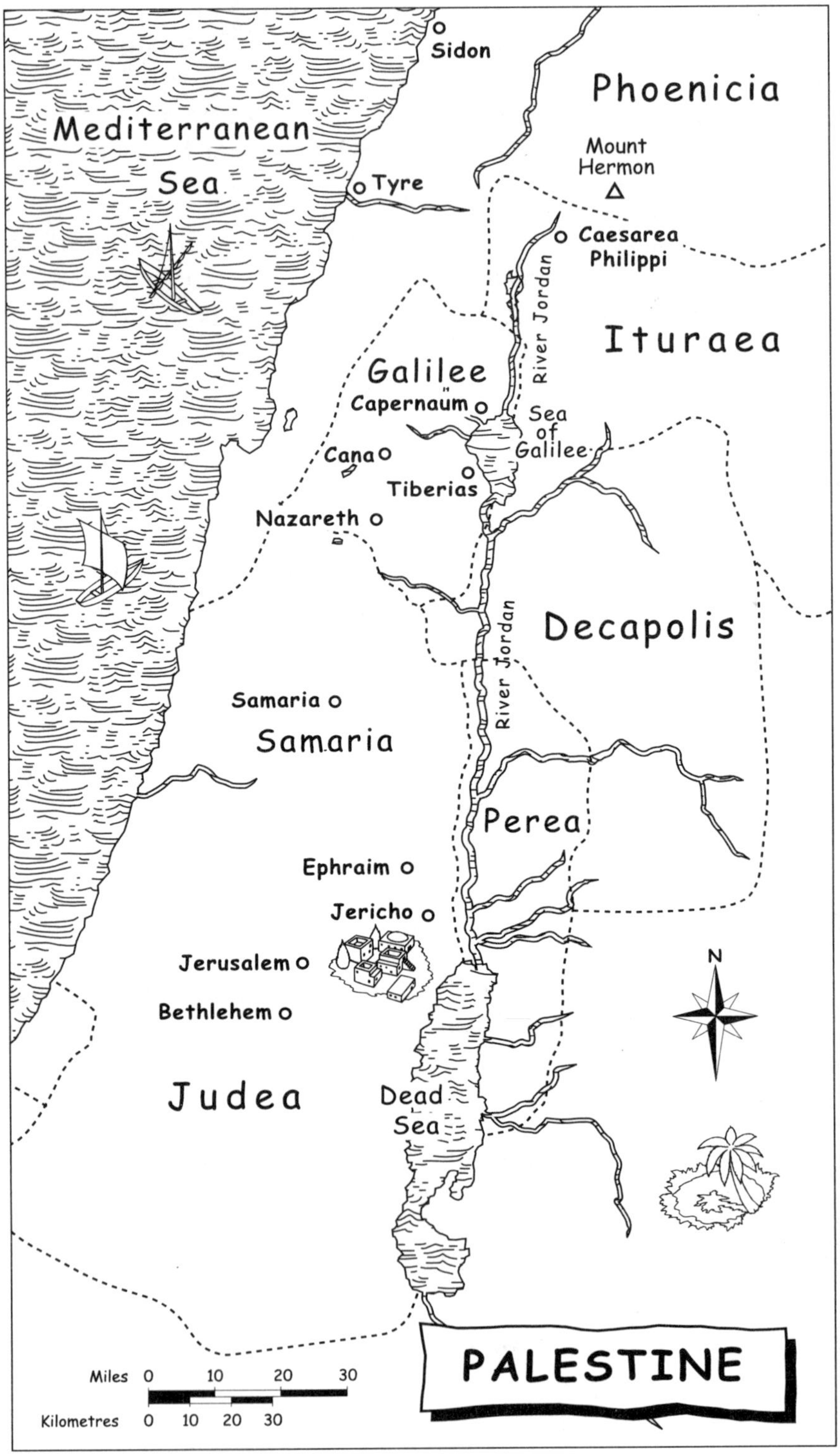

FACTSHEET 2 The River Jordan

The name of the River Jordan gives us a clue as to the kind of river it was. The name means 'the river that rushes down' and that is just what the River Jordan did. After leaving the mountains in the north it tumbled down the valley very quickly. It soon arrived in the Sea (or Lake) of Galilee. This beautiful freshwater lake was the main area for fishing in Palestine. It was close to this lake that Jesus was born and spent most of his early years. The lake was well-known for its sudden storms.

When the river left the Sea of Galilee it cut a deep, winding valley. The temperature from here to the Dead Sea was so high that few people lived in or travelled through the area. The Dead Sea, at the bottom of the River Jordan, was long and narrow (48 miles by 10 miles) and without an outlet. As the water could not escape so the sea filled with salt and minerals. It was so salty that fish could only live in its waters for a few minutes. Nothing was able to grow on its banks. The salt on the banks was collected and sold to the few people who lived there. They used it to season and preserve their food.

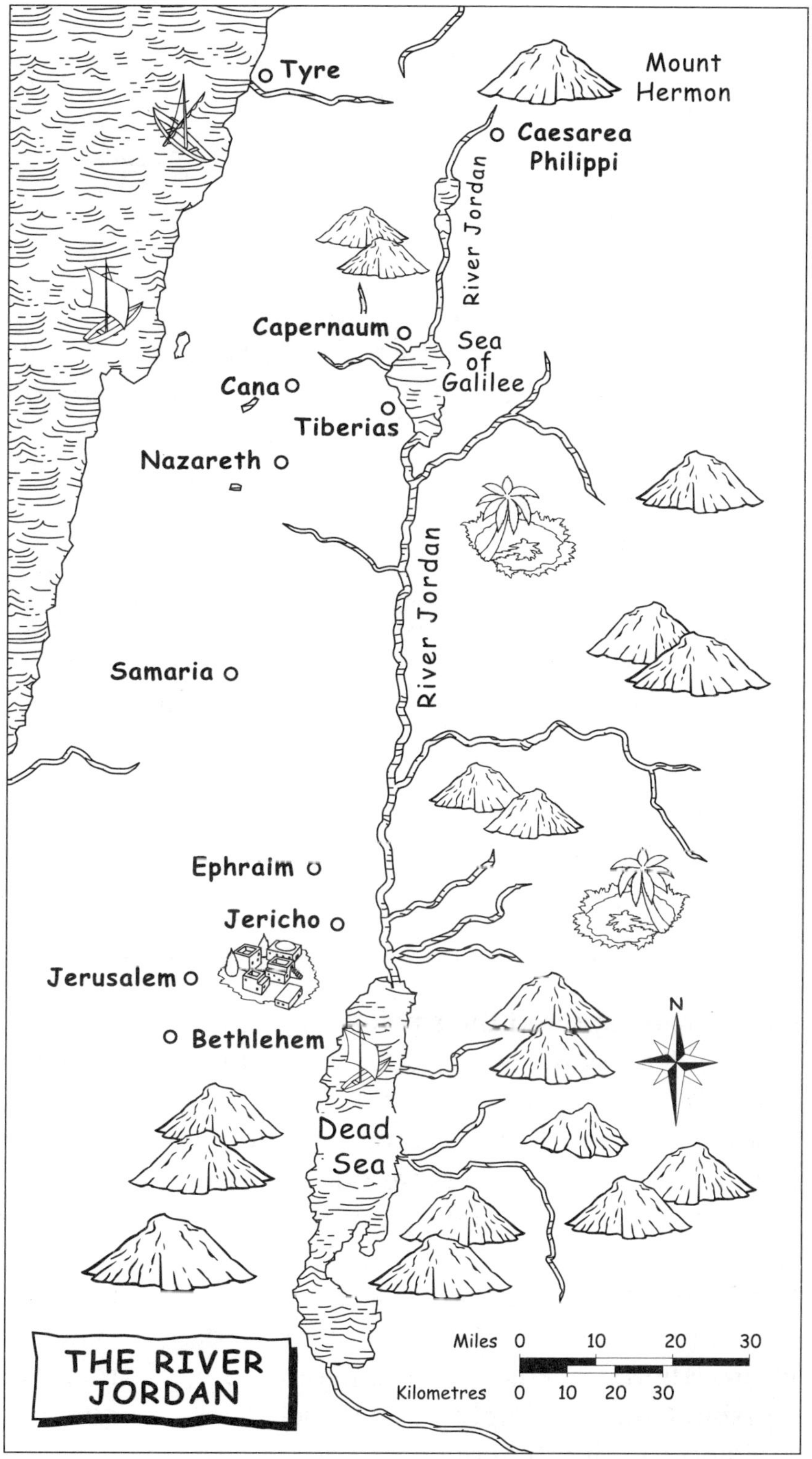

See Matthew 2.2; 5.13; 27.55; Luke 3.3

FACTSHEET 3 Jerusalem

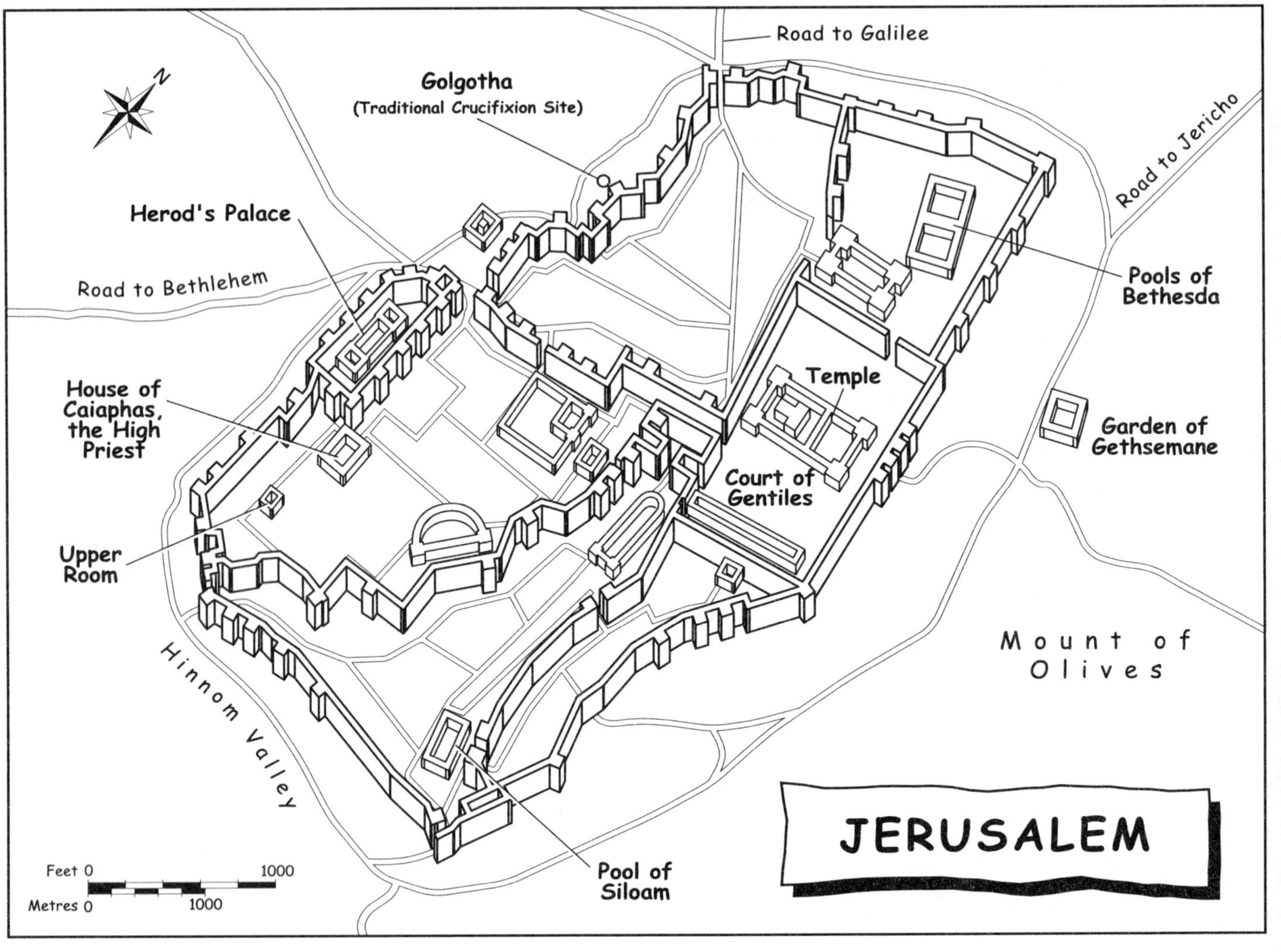

King David captured the small hilltop town of Jerusalem some 3,000 years ago. It was in such a good position that he made it his capital city. Solomon, his son, built a beautiful Temple there but this was later destroyed by an army from Babylon. The Temple lay in ruins for over 500 years. Just before Jesus was born King Herod began to rebuild it. He was not interested in providing a building for the people to worship God. He simply wanted the building to bring him great praise. He also built a palace for himself in Jerusalem. About 50,000 people lived in this noisy and busy city when Jesus was alive.

The streets of Jerusalem were very narrow and steep. The best way to get around the city was by walking. But some people used camels, donkeys or horses. Traders were to be seen on almost every street corner selling their goods. There were also several markets in the city. People came to them from the villages around Jerusalem. When there was a religious festival so many people came to the city that you could hardly move.

See Luke 13.33-35; 19.28, 37

FACTSHEET 4 The Romans in Palestine

In 63 BC the Roman General, Pompey, entered Palestine at the head of his army and conquered Jerusalem. This was a great blow to the people. The Romans destroyed many of their holy buildings. They made them pay very heavy taxes. The Romans gave them a ruler instead of letting them rule themselves. When Jesus was born the ruler was King Herod who was very cruel. By the time Jesus died the ruler was Pontius Pilate. It was Pilate who ordered that Jesus be put to death.

The Romans stationed 3,000 soldiers, a legion, in Palestine. The whole legion was controlled by a legate. Each legion was then made up of ten cohorts and each of these was commanded by a tribune. In each cohort there were three centuries and each of these was led by a centurion. The centurions were chosen from amongst the older Roman soldiers. Centurions were very important. They carried out the will of the Roman Emperor in Rome. Their wages were about fifteen times greater than that paid to ordinary soldiers. They were expected to lead and train the men under their command.

See Matthew 8.5; Luke 3.14

FACTSHEET 5 Religious groups

In the time of Jesus the rabbis taught the Holy Scriptures to the people. They also spent a lot of time talking amongst themselves about the different Jewish laws. On one famous occasion they spent hours wondering whether a Jew should eat an egg which a chicken had laid on the Sabbath day.

The name 'Pharisee' means 'Separated one' and this gives us a clue about how the Pharisees lived. They were the leading Jewish group at the time. There were 6,000 Pharisees in Palestine. They tried to live holy and separate lives. They tried not to cooperate with the Romans. Jewish people went to them for advice about the many laws they were expected to follow.

The Sadducees were another important group in Palestine. Most of the Sadducees were wealthy men. Most of the Jewish religious leaders came from this group of people. The High Priest, for example, was usually a Sadducee. Together with the Pharisees the Sadducees formed the Sanhedrin. This was the most important Jewish Council. The Sanhedrin had seventy members. It met in Herod's Temple in Jerusalem. It could punish people who were found guilty of committing a crime.

See Matthew 5.20; 16.1; 22.23-32; Mark 8.15; 12.18; Luke 11.39

FACTSHEET 6 The Temple

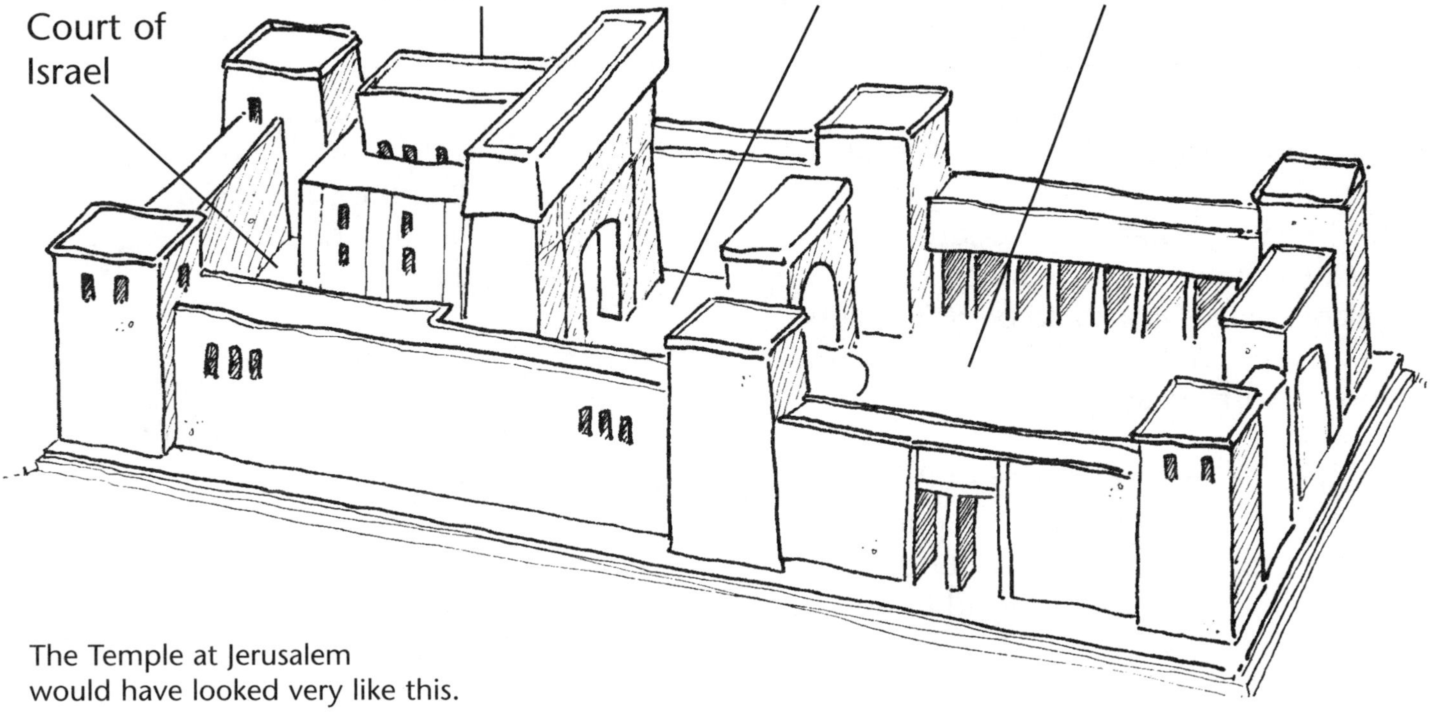

The Temple at Jerusalem would have looked very like this.

It was King Solomon who had first built a Temple in Jerusalem. Jews came from all over Israel to worship God there. The Temple was destroyed by the Babylonians in 586 BC. For over 500 years, little attempt was made to rebuild it. Then, in 19 BC, King Herod started to build a new Temple. He died in 4 BC but the Temple was not finished until AD 56. Then, in AD 70, the Romans completely destroyed it. It was never rebuilt after that.

As you can see from the illustration, there were several courts around the Temple itself. Everyone was allowed to go into the first courtyard – the Court of the Gentiles (non-Jews). Jewish men and women were allowed into the second courtyard – the Court of the Women. There were thirteen boxes, shaped like trumpets, in this courtyard. Jewish people placed their offerings to the Temple in one of these boxes.

Only Jewish men could go further into the Court of Israel. Priests alone were allowed into the final court – the Court of the Priests. A large stone altar stood in front of the Temple building. It was here that animals were killed as sacrifices. Twelve steps led up to the Temple itself. Inside, a pair of heavy curtains stood in front of the Holy of Holies. Only the High Priest, once a year, was able to enter this place.

See Matthew 4.5-6; 12.6; Mark 13.1

FACTSHEET 7 The Synagogue

The word 'synagogue' means 'a meeting place'. It is the place where Jewish men, women and children worship. By the time of Jesus there were synagogues in every town and village in Palestine. The city of Jerusalem alone had 394 synagogues. The Jewish law allowed a synagogue to be built if there were ten married men in a village. No service could be held unless ten men were there. This is still true for most Jewish synagogues today.

Each synagogue chose one of their men to be the rabbi. The rabbi taught the people about how to live a good, Jewish life. As the rabbi was not paid to do this he had another job as well. Any male over the age of 13 could be asked to read from the scroll or lead the prayers in a service. Synagogues were open each day for prayers. The leaders of the synagogue sat on the seats in front of the Ark. The scrolls of the Law, called the Torah, were kept in the Ark and only brought out for someone to read from them.

Women, girls and younger boys sat together in the balcony or behind a screen. They did not play any part in the service. The synagogue was also used as a school. Both adults and children were taught there.

Matthew 12.9; Mark 6.2; Luke 4.15, 16

The large synagogue at Capernaum would have looked very like this.

FACTSHEET 8 — The Sabbath day

Jewish people have always rested from work for one day each week. This day, the Sabbath day, begins at sunset on Friday evening. It ends when the first three stars appear in the sky on Saturday evening. Jews are following the example of God. After spending six days creating the world God rested on the seventh. The day began and ended with a trumpet being blown.

Before the Sabbath day starts, all homes are cleaned and food is cooked. No cooking is done on the Sabbath day. Everyone bathes and puts on their best clothes. The lamps are lit and the whole family sits down to eat a meal together. Before the meal starts the father blesses his wife and children.

Everyone goes to the synagogue for a service on Saturday morning. There are readings from the Holy Scriptures, the rabbi teaches and there are prayers. In the past, everyone walked to and from the synagogue and many people still do. The Sabbath laws applied to everything and everyone in Palestine. The Sabbath was also a day of rest for servants and even for animals. People could only take a 'Sabbath day's journey' (about 2,000 footsteps).

Jewish laws allowed people to deal with an emergency on the Sabbath day. Farmers were allowed to pull their animals out of a ditch. Doctors could help sick people. If a person's, or an animal's, life was in danger they could be saved. Everything else was work and not allowed.

See Matthew 12.2; Mark 2.27; 3.2

FACTSHEET 9 Places in the Gospels

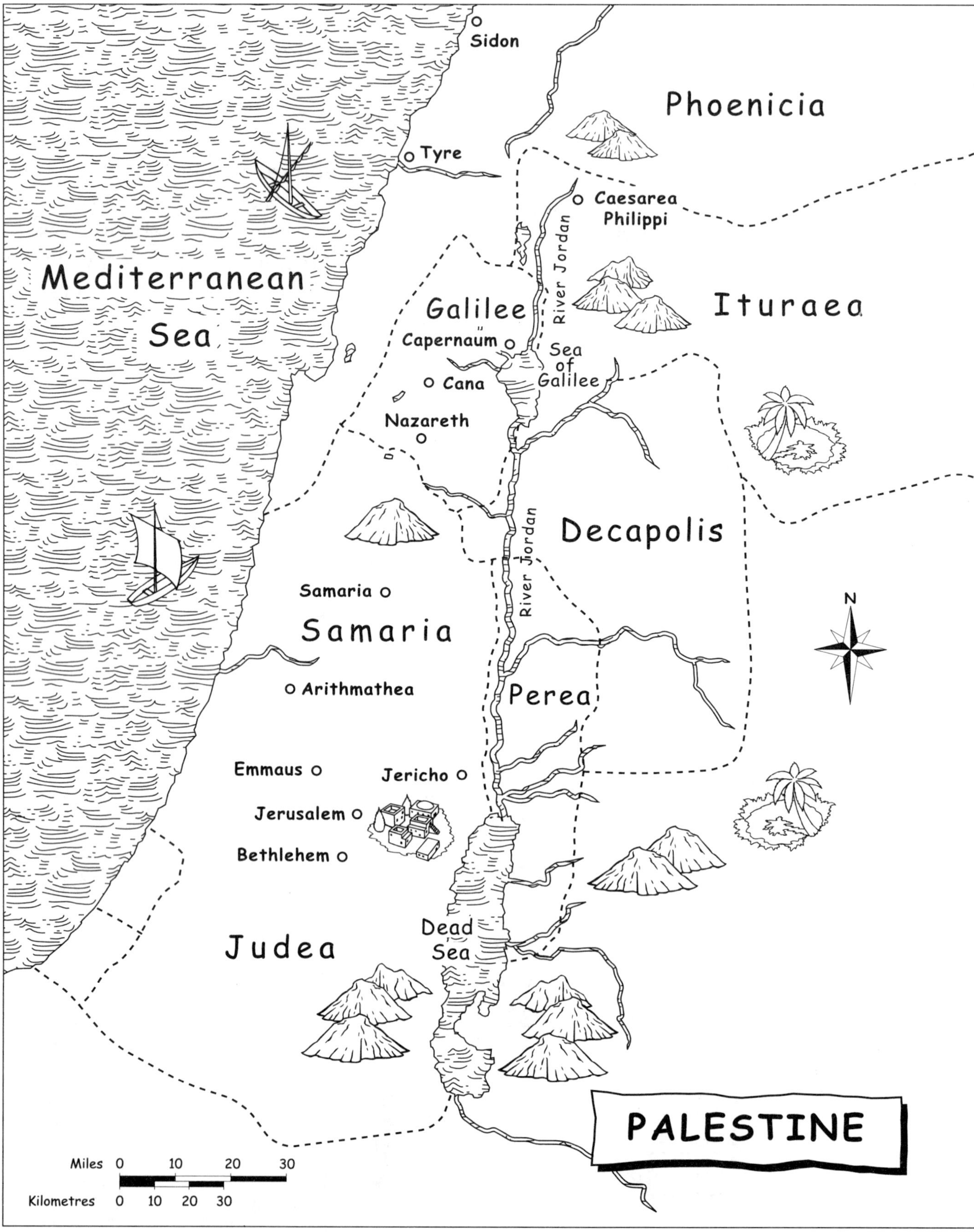

FACTSHEET 10 Houses

In the time of Jesus, most Jewish families lived in one-roomed houses. These were usually built out of mud-bricks. Heavy wooden beams were laid across the tops of the walls. Smaller planks of wood were then laid across these beams. Brushwood, reeds, mud and grass were placed on top. (See also Factsheet 20.) The roof-top of the house was flat. Women did many of their jobs on the roof. The whole family could relax there at the end of the day.

Inside the house the only room was divided into two parts. The floor was usually dirt or clay. The family's goats or sheep lived here. A fire was lit in a hole in the floor and the smoke went out of the door. At one end of the room there was a platform. This was where the family ate, worked and slept. At night, straw mats were laid on the floor. People slept in their day clothes. A lamp was kept alight at all times. It was placed on a special shelf which was cut into a wall or suspended from the ceiling.

See Matthew 5.14-16; Mark 2.1-12; Luke 11.5-8

FACTSHEET 11 Clothes

At the time of Jesus, men and women wore similar clothes in Palestine. They wore an inner garment with another tunic on top. New tunics were sold in the market-place without a hole for the head. This showed that nobody else had worn them. The outer garment was called the 'colobium'. Jewish people liked to wear bright colours. There was usually a stripe from the top to the bottom of the colobium.

Most people wore woollen clothes. The clothes of poor people were sometimes made out of hair-cloth. This was very rough and uncomfortable to wear. The clothes of rich people were made out of linen or silk. These clothes were much softer. The finest clothes were white.

Many people had 'best clothes' as well as everyday clothes. They wore their best clothes on the Sabbath day.

People wore simple sandals on their feet. These had a leather base and were tied to the feet by a thong. A square of material was folded crossways and worn on the head by men and women. The material fell down the back of the neck. This protected people from the blazing sun. Everyone also had a cloak. They wore this when it became colder at night. They also put it over themselves like a blanket when they went to sleep.

See Matthew 6.19, 25; 22.11-13; Luke 15.22; 16.19

FACTSHEET 12 Food

During the time of Jesus, Jewish people ate simple meals. Bread was the main food. It was shaped into round, flat buns. In the heat it quickly went dry and mouldy. Fresh bread was baked every two days. This was one of the most important jobs carried out by the women in the family. The bread was broken in the hands and shared between everyone.

Fruit was a very important source of food. Sometimes the grapes were eaten as fast as they were harvested. Usually, however, they were laid out in the sun and dried. They were eaten later as raisins. Figs, grapes and apricots were eaten fresh from the tree. Soup was often made from vegetables and pulses. Beans, onions, garlic and leeks were plentiful.

Meat was a luxury. If a guest was expected then mutton, lamb or goat might be added to the evening's stew. Jewish people have strict laws about eating meat. They can only eat animals which eat grass and have cloven hoofs. They cannot eat pork. Fish was an important food in the time of Jesus. It was salted or dried. Jewish people cannot eat shellfish.

There were usually two meals a day. The times that these were eaten varied with different families. The evening meal was the only time that the family sat down to eat together. The most important meal was eaten at the start of the Sabbath day.

See Matthew 26.26; John 2.1-12; 21.12

FACTSHEET 13 Family life

In the time of Jesus, most Jewish people lived in large families. The family at home included grandparents, aunts, uncles and cousins as well as parents and children. Servants were also a part of many families. Everyone, from the youngest upwards, had their own work to do in the family.

The man was the head of the family. His wife called him 'Master'. He was expected to guide the rest of the family. The older women taught the younger ones how to look after the family. Children were expected to collect firewood for the fire, keep the lamps alight and look after the animals. Children were expected to obey their parents and do as they were told. The animals lived with the family in the house. Men taught their trade to their sons. The father of Jesus, Joseph, was a carpenter. Jesus was a carpenter until he was 30 years old.

Women in Palestine had a very busy life. Starting before dawn broke in the morning, they made bread, fetched the water, looked after the children, made goods and often sold the family's produce in the market as well.

See Matthew 5.31,32; 19.3-9; Luke 1.28

FACTSHEET 14 Farming

The plough which farmers used was a simple wooden stake. It had a handle for the farmer to hold and a point of iron which ran through the earth. The plough was pulled by one or more oxen. A yoke held the oxen together. This made sure that they walked in the same direction. The farmer controlled the oxen with a long pole.

Farmers sowed their seed in Palestine by 'broadcasting'. This meant that they carried the seed in a bag and walked along tossing it to the right and the left. They took little care where the seed landed. Much of the seed was wasted. It fell on paths and stony ground as well as good earth.

Everyone in the family helped at harvest time. Harvesting started in April after the March rains. The farmer held the grain in one hand and cut it at the bottom with a sickle. Then it was gathered into bundles or sheaves. The sheaves were loaded on a cart. A donkey pulled the cart to a level piece of ground. The crops had to be threshed to separate the grains from the stalks. To do this the farmer beat the sheaves with sticks. Then in the evening, when a wind was blowing, the threshed corn was thrown into the air. The grain fell to the ground. The stalks, or chaff, which were lighter were blown away in the wind.

See Matthew 3.11-12; 9.37; 13.1-9; 23.23

FACTSHEET 15 Fishing

Most of the fishing in Palestine was done in the Sea of Galilee. There were more than twenty different kinds of fish found there. On a calm day you would have found at least three hundred boats fishing there. At least seven of the twelve disciples of Jesus were fishermen.

The life of a fisherman in Palestine was hard and dangerous. A stormy night's fishing would be followed by a day spent sorting and selling the fish. Usually there were nets to be mended as well. Boats often worked in pairs. Often a father would work one boat and his sons the other. They stretched a large drag-net between the two boats. After the fish swam into the net it was tightened and pulled aboard. Sometimes the catch was so heavy that the net broke.

When Jesus called Peter and Andrew to follow him they were casting their nets into the water. Fishermen did this when they knew that there was a shoal of fish close to land. The nets that they used were circular with weights attached to the edges. They were thrown over the swimming fish close to land. As the net sank down in the water so the fish were trapped. It was important that the net was gathered in without the fish escaping.

See Matthew 13.47,48; Mark 1.20; Luke 5.5

FACTSHEET 16 Marriage

In Palestine, in the time of Jesus, people were usually young when they married. Their parents arranged for them to marry. The man's father paid the girl's family a 'bride price'. The girl's family also paid a dowry (a sum of money given to the groom on marriage). The two people were now engaged. After some months, or years, the two married.

Great care was taken over preparing a bride for her wedding. Her hair was plaited and lengths of silk woven into the plaits. Coins were attached to the silk plaits. A girl could have more than a thousand coins in her hair. Her face was polished until it shone. Her nails, hands and feet were polished with henna. Her eyebrows were pencilled in until they met. Her eyelids were blackened.

Before the bridegroom left his home to collect his bride a garland was put around his neck. Along the journey, he was met by women holding lamps. Great care was taken to keep the lamps alight. The bride wore a long white dress and a long coat. She was taken back to the bridegroom's house. During the service he lifted her veil. This might have been the first time that they had seen each other.

The feast that followed might go on for several days. At the end of it the guests went home. They were very tired but happy. They prayed that God would bless the groom and his bride in the future.

See Matthew 1.19; 25.1-10; John 2.1-12

FACTSHEET 17 Education

Every child's education began at home. Boys were taught by their mothers until they were five or six years old. At that age they were sent to school in the local synagogue. Mothers taught their daughters at home until they left to be married.

The teacher in the synagogue sat on a low platform and the children gathered around his feet. Each boy was given a small wooden tablet, covered with wax, on which to write. The teacher said something to the children and the children repeated it many times until they had learned it.

The father took a great interest in the religious education of his sons. He taught them the beliefs of the Jewish people. He also taught them to remember passages from the Scriptures. At the age of 13, a Jewish boy becomes an adult. To celebrate this he still goes through a special service in the synagogue. This is called a Bar Mitzvah. At this service he reads, from the scrolls of the Law in Hebrew.

In the past, when they started to work, boys were likely to follow in their father's footsteps. He taught them his own skills. They could continue the family business when their father was too old to work. Jewish children were expected to look after their parents when they grew old.

See Luke 2.41-52

FACTSHEET 18 Death

In the time of Jesus, as soon as someone in a Jewish family had died, his or her eyelids were closed. Members of the family made a tear in the clothes that they were wearing. This showed how upset they were at the person's death. They then put on a rough coat of sackcloth. They wore this until the person had been buried. They often poured dirt and ashes on their own head. This was another sign of respect.

Poor people could not afford to have their own tombs (places in which the dead were buried). Instead their bodies were carried to the Kidron Valley, outside Jerusalem, and thrown into the valley, where a fire was always kept alight.

But richer people made sure that they had built a tomb before they died. This tomb was cut out of the rock on a hillside. The body was taken to the tomb, wrapped in a white cloth and the face was covered with a separate cloth. The hands and the feet were bandaged. The body was then laid on a ledge in the tomb.

Wild animals roved the hillside at night and so the tomb had to be sealed. A groove was cut in the earth across the entrance to the tomb. A large, circular rock was rolled along the groove until it covered the entrance. It would take more than one man to roll the rock into place.

See Matthew 27.7; John 19.40; 20.5; 20.7

FACTSHEET 19 Jewish festivals

During the time of Jesus, religious festivals were a very important part of life for Jewish people. These festivals took place at important times in the farming year. They also looked back to important events in Jewish history. Jewish people came from all over the Roman Empire to celebrate the festivals of Passover, Tabernacles and Weeks in Jerusalem.

The most important festival, still celebrated, is Passover. This looks back to the time when the Jews left slavery in Egypt. Moses had led them across the desert for 40 years. He died just as they were about to enter their Promised Land, Canaan. Jewish people are reminded of this journey by the special food that they eat during the festival. It was during this festival that Jesus died.

50 days after Passover begins there is a harvest festival (the Feast of Weeks). At this time farmers used to offer the first of the year's crop to God. They brought two loaves of leavened (risen) bread as a gift.

A little while later, in September/October, comes the festival of Tabernacles. Every Jewish family built their own booth in the house or garden. They lived in them for eight days. The roofs of the huts were decorated with leaves, fruits and vegetables. When Jewish people travelled in the desert for 40 years they lived in huts or tents. God looked after them. At this festival they thank God for doing this.

See Matthew 26.17-21;
Mark 14.1,2;
John 7.1-13

FACTSHEET 20 Building

There was always a great deal of building going on in Palestinian towns and villages. As the population kept getting bigger there was a constant need for new houses. For security reasons, city walls were frequently extended and strengthened. Wells were dug to ensure a constant supply of fresh water whilst cisterns were built to share the water.

Building a house

First bricks had to be made to build the house. A shallow pit was dug and filled with clay and water, then chopped straw was added as a binder. The ingredients were mixed by people walking on them, and then pressed into wooden moulds. The bricks were set out in the sun to dry and then cemented into place using a trowel, a wooden square and a 'plumbline'. Finally, the walls of the building were put up and wooden beams were laid across the top. Smaller beams were then laid across these beams. Over the top of this, layers of brushwood, reeds, mud and grass were placed. The roof of the house was flat.

Similar building techniques are still used in many Middle Eastern countries today.

Building a water tunnel

Water tunnels were built in the larger towns so that an opposing army could not cut off the water supply during a siege. Two groups of workers dug their way towards each other, shouting at the tops of their voices. They did this to make sure their two tunnels met in the middle.

John the Baptist

AIMS

The aims of this section are to introduce:

1 John the Baptist (the forerunner of Jesus)

2 The birth of John the Baptist and John's links with Jesus

3 The preaching and baptism of John the Baptist.

KEY WORDS

Abraham	Herod
Angel	Holy Spirit
Annas	Jerusalem
Baptism	Messiah
Caiaphas	Pontius Pilate
Circumcision	Temple

Matthew 3.1-12; Mark 1.1-8; Luke 1.5-25; John 1.19-28

1 John the Baptist was born around 7 BC to Zechariah, a priest working in the Temple in Jerusalem, and Elizabeth. The couple were elderly and childless. Zechariah was told by an angel that he would father a child. He was told that the child would be great in God's sight and be filled with the Holy Spirit from birth. He would bring many of the people of Israel back to God.

Above all else John would prepare the people for the coming of Jesus. He would be the forerunner. The forerunner was a familiar sight in Israel, preparing the people in the crowd for the coming of any important religious dignitary.

2 After his birth the Gospels are silent about John until he appeared as a wild preacher living in the desert. His message to the people was, "Turn away from your sins and be baptized, and God will forgive you." (Luke 3.3).

He told the people that if they had two shirts, they must share with the person who had none. Tax collectors were to collect no more money than was legal. Soldiers were told not to take money from anyone. Those who were sorry for their sins went to John to be baptized in the River Jordan.

THE STORIES

1 Zechariah and his wife, Elizabeth, were very old. They didn't have any children. An angel appeared to Zechariah and told him that Elizabeth would have a son. The son would have a special job to do. He was going to prepare the people for the coming of Jesus. Everyone in Elizabeth's village was very excited.

2 We do not know anything about John as he grew up. But suddenly we find him living in the desert wearing a coat made out of animal skins. He only ate locusts and wild honey. The people were so fascinated by John that they walked into the desert to see him. They wanted to hear what he had to say. He told them that they must be baptized in the River Jordan. To be baptized they must be dipped beneath the water. After this they were to go home and live a better life. Jesus was one of those baptized by John.

DISCUSSION POINTS

1 *The custom of a forerunner smoothing the path ahead for someone important.* Why was the forerunner there? What was he expected to do?

2 *The arrival of a new baby in the family.* Why are people so excited by this? What was special about the birth of John? How do neighbours and friends share in the excitement of a birth?

3 *The importance of washing.* What happens if we do not wash? Why did people come to John to be baptized? What did the people hope for?

 NAME..

Zechariah and Elizabeth

Read Luke 1.57-66.

What did the angel tell Zechariah?

Why were Elizabeth's friends happy?

What was Zechariah's son going to do?

When did Zechariah begin to speak?

The birth of Jesus

AIMS

The aims of this section are to introduce:

1 The visit of the angel to Joseph

2 The visit of the angel to Mary

3 The journey of Mary to see Elizabeth

4 The birth of Jesus.

KEY WORDS

Angel	Joseph
Bethlehem	Luke
Church	Magnificat
Elizabeth	Mary
Gabriel	Matthew
Herod	Messiah
Holy Spirit	Palestine
Jesus	

Matthew 1.18-25; Luke 1.26-2.5

1 It is Matthew who records the visit of 'the angel of the Lord' to Joseph. Joseph's dilemma was that he was only engaged to be married to Mary when the angel told him that she was pregnant. Matthew tells us that Joseph was a man who "always did what was right" and in the climate of the time this would normally mean breaking his agreement to marry Mary. At the same time he did not want to bring public disgrace on her. The angel, knowing his dilemma, told Joseph that Mary's child had been conceived by the Holy Spirit.

In Luke, the birth of Jesus is announced to Mary by the angel Gabriel. Mary is deeply worried by the angel's appearance and even more so when she is told that she is to be the mother of 'the Christ' (the Messiah). Again, she is assured that God will be the 'father' of the child. Mary's song of praise, the Magnificat, is used in many Roman Catholic and Anglican services.

2 The birth of Jesus took place in a stable. Matthew hardly mentions this and our details come from Luke's account. The exact date for the event cannot be determined. Matthew and Luke both agree that King Herod was still ruling Palestine when Jesus was born. We know from contemporary sources that he died in 4/5 BC. The most likely date for the birth of Jesus is, therefore, 5/6 BC. Matthew tells us that Joseph, Mary and the infant Jesus, returned from Egypt when they heard that Herod had died.

THE STORIES

1 You will often read in the Bible about angels appearing to people. They were sent by God to carry important messages. The most important of the angels was called Gabriel. One day he was sent by God to carry a message to a young teenage girl called Mary. Although she was only young, Mary was already engaged to marry Joseph, who was probably much older than she was. The angel took Mary completely by surprise. He told her that she had been chosen by God for a very important job. She was going to give birth to Jesus, God's Son. Jesus was going to set up God's Kingdom on earth.

2 When Mary's baby was almost due, the Roman Emperor issued an order. He wanted to count every person in Palestine. He could then make sure that they were paying their taxes. He said that everyone had to return to the village in which they, or their husband, had been born. Mary and Joseph went home to Bethlehem. When they arrived, Mary knew that her baby was going to be born very soon. Joseph searched everywhere for an inn in which she could have her baby. All of the inns were full. In the end, the baby was born in a stable.

DISCUSSION POINTS

1 *The impact that the birth of a new baby has on a family.* What are the necessary preparations for the birth? What are the responsibilities of having a baby?

2 *The differences between the birth of Jesus and the birth of a baby today.*

3 *The story of the birth of Jesus in Luke's Gospel.*

4 *Making a crib.* Discuss the figures placed in the crib.

 NAME..

The land of Jesus

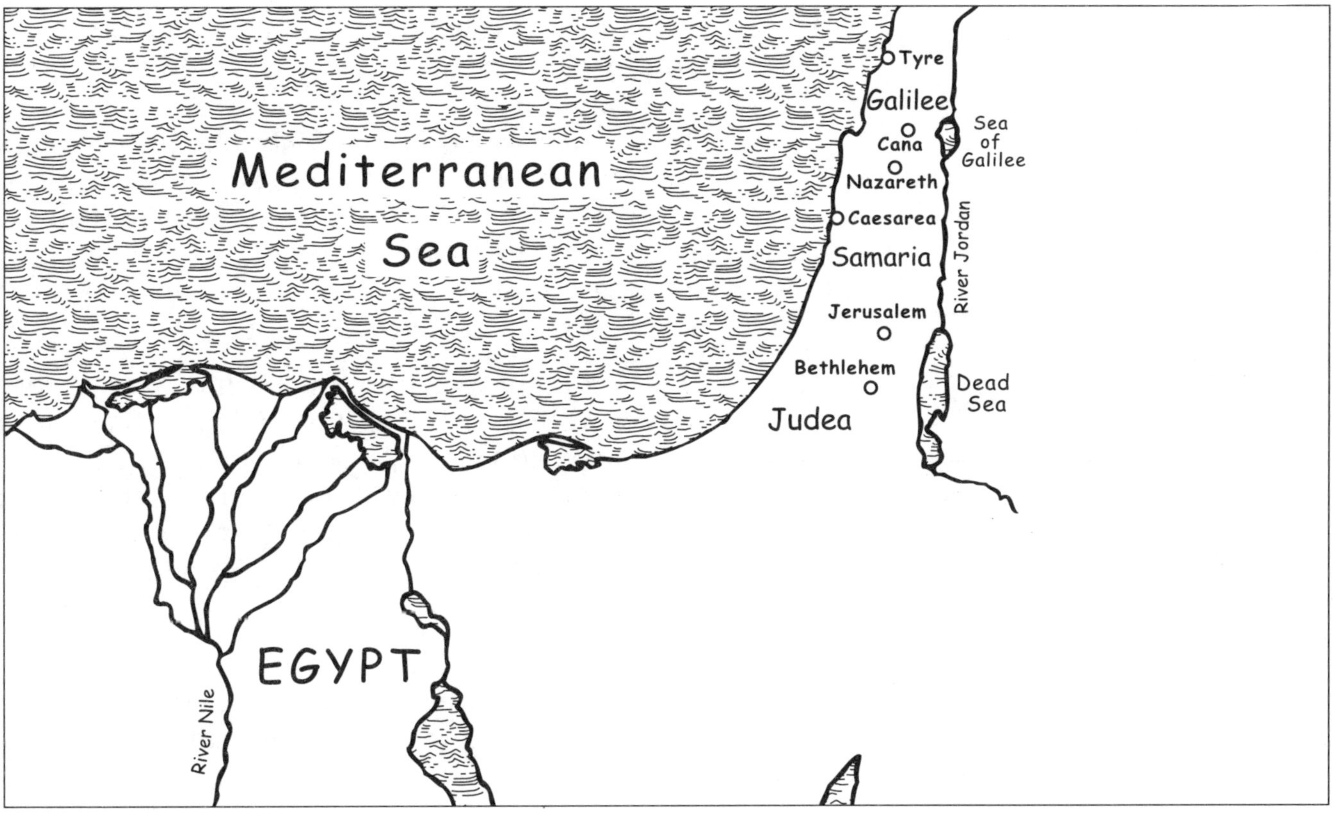

Read Matthew 2.13, 2.19-23 and Luke 2.1-7.

Put a circle around and label:

1. The place from which Mary and Joseph travelled to be counted

2. The village in which Jesus was born

3. The place to which the family travelled to escape Herod

4. The place in which Herod lived

5. The area in which Joseph brought Jesus up.

The shepherds

AIMS

The aims of this section are to introduce:

1 The announcement of the birth of Jesus to the shepherds

2 The visit of the shepherds to the infant Jesus

3 What happened after the shepherds made their visit

4 The symbolic importance of the shepherds in the birth stories.

KEY WORDS

Angel	Joseph
Elizabeth	Magnificat
Gabriel	Mary
Holy Spirit	Nazareth

Luke 2.8-20

1 The occupation of shepherd in first century Palestine was very low status. Shepherds were considered to be untrustworthy, whilst their occupation made them religiously unclean. They were social outcasts. Such were the people to whom the Gospel (the Good News of Jesus's birth) was first given and this theme is repeated many times in Luke's Gospel. In both the Old and New Testaments, shepherds symbolise ordinary people who joyfully receive God's gift.

2 The announcement of the birth of Jesus to the shepherds uses many of the words which are most prominent in Luke's Gospel ('good news', 'Saviour' and 'Lord'). This shows how important the angelic announcement was. The time had come for the Messiah's arrival on earth to be announced.

3 The verse 'Glory to God in the highest' is the climax of the story. Its two parts relate to heaven and earth. The peace which the Messiah brings is given to those to whom God also gives His grace.

THE STORY

There were shepherds everywhere in Palestine because there were so many sheep. Flocks of sheep with their shepherds were to be found on almost every hillside. On a very special night, God's angel appeared to some shepherds just outside Bethlehem. They were very frightened when this happened but the angel told them not to be afraid. He was bringing them some very good news. Their Saviour had just been born and, if they travelled to Bethlehem, they would find him in a manger. Suddenly the single angel was surrounded by many more and they were all singing a song of praise to God.

When the angels returned to heaven the shepherds travelled to Bethlehem so that they could see the baby. The journey didn't take very long. They soon found Mary and Joseph with the baby lying in a manger. The shepherds told Mary and Joseph what the angels had said. Then the shepherds went out to tell everyone else. All who heard the story were amazed. But Mary was quiet and thoughtful about it all. The shepherds returned home to their flocks praising God as they went.

DISCUSSION POINTS

1 *The story of the angels appearing to the shepherds.*

2 *The life of a first century Palestinian shepherd.* Children can discuss what dangers and problems there might be for a shepherd so many years ago (e.g. wild animals, the elements, poverty).

3 *The likely reaction of the shepherds to the appearance of an angel.*

4 *Mary's reaction to the events.* She remembered and thought deeply about the events. Compare this with a similar comment in Luke 2.51.

COPYMASTER 3 NAME..

The shepherds visit Jesus

Read Luke 2.8-20

What were the shepherds doing?

What did the angel tell them?

What did the shepherds decide to do?

What did the shepherds find in Bethlehem?

What did the shepherds do after they had seen Jesus?

The Wise Men

AIMS

The aims of this section are to introduce:

1 The story of the Wise Men visiting the infant Jesus

2 The star by which the Wise Men were miraculously directed

3 The reason why the visit of the Wise Men was important in the Gospel story.

KEY WORDS

Bethlehem	Magi
David	Mary
Frankincense	Messiah
Herod	Myrrh
Jerusalem	

Matthew 2.1-12

1 Bethlehem was only a tiny village but its importance in Jewish history and religion far outweighed its size. It was the place where Jacob buried Rachel (Genesis 35.19), where Ruth met Boaz (Ruth 1.22-2.6) and, most importantly, it was the place where King David was born. For Christians it was the place where the angelic host announced the birth of Jesus (Luke 2.8-20).

2 The Wise Men in Matthew's story cannot be identified with any certainty. The term covered a wide cross-section of men who studied astrology, dreams, magic and books thought to contain prophecies about the future. Probably these men had studied the old Jewish holy books and astrological predictions. Their studies had brought them to Bethlehem. There is no extra-biblical evidence for the star that they are said to have seen and followed.

3 Bringing gifts was a particularly important social custom in the Near East. Frankincense is a gum whilst myrrh is a highly valued spice and perfume obtained from a tree. Clearly, gold is special because expensive. The fact that the Wise Men brought three gifts does not necessarily imply that there were three of them, although it may do so.

THE STORY

Jesus was born in Bethlehem during the time when the very cruel King Herod was on the throne. In a country a long way from Bethlehem there were men who spent all of their time studying the stars and holy books. These men were known as 'Magi'. One day, the Magi noticed a star in the sky. They hadn't seen it before. They thought it was a special star which might lead them to the place where a very special person was born. They set out to follow the star.

They followed it to Jerusalem. When they got there they went straight to Herod's palace. They asked him where the new king was so that they might worship him. Herod was very angry. He was frightened to hear them speak of a new king. He wanted to be the only king. He called together the Jewish leaders and asked them where this new king would be. They told him that he would be born in Bethlehem and Herod passed this on to the Magi. Herod told the Magi to let him know when they found the new baby. He didn't tell them he was planning to kill Jesus. The men followed the star until it stopped over the manger where Jesus lay. They entered and found Jesus with Mary, his mother. They bowed down in front of him and gave him their gifts of gold, frankincense and myrrh.

DISCUSSION POINTS

1 *The Bible story of the Wise Men visiting Jesus.*

2 *The importance of stars.* You can talk about how some people believe in astrological predictions.

3 *The importance of the gifts that the Magi brought to Jesus.* Why do gifts matter? What do they show? Did the Magi's gifts have any special meaning? (Children can be encouraged to research this.)

COPYMASTER 4 NAME..

The Magi

Read Matthew 2.1-12.

Draw the Magi (Wise Men) travelling across the desert to find Jesus. What did they look like? What were they wearing? What were they riding?

What did the men say to Herod?

What did Herod say to the men?

What did the Magi (Wise Men) do when they found Jesus?

Jesus grows up

AIMS

The aims of this section are to introduce:

1 The very important Jewish festival of Passover (Pesach)

2 The Jewish ceremony of barmitzvah

3 The Jewish upbringing of Jesus

4 The encounter of Jesus with the leaders of his own community

5 The awareness of Jesus that God had sent him to earth with a special job to do.

KEY WORDS

Barmitzvah	Pesach
Exodus	Sabbath Day
Jerusalem	Synagogue
Joseph	Temple
Mary	Torah
Messiah	

Luke 2.41-52

1 There were three Jewish festivals each year that drew Jewish people from all over the Roman Empire to Jerusalem. The most important of these festivals was, and is, Passover, or Pesach. The festival commemorates the escape (the exodus) of the Jews from slavery in Egypt.

2 While Jesus was a child he would have stayed at home but when he was 12 he was taken by his parents to the Temple in Jerusalem for the first time. In the Jewish faith of the time, 12 was the age for a boy's barmitzvah, although it is now 13. It is customary in this service for the boy to read from the scroll of the Torah (the Law) in the synagogue. This is done for the first time on the Sabbath day after the boy's 13th birthday. Barmitzvah means 'son of the commandments'.

3 The first visit of Jesus to the synagogue, and the reaction of the leaders of his community to it, is to be seen in the light of the overall mission of Jesus. Luke wants his readers to understand that not only was Jesus God's long promised Messiah but also that Jesus was conscious of his unique destiny from a very early age.

THE STORY

Every year, Mary and Joseph, the parents of Jesus, paid a special visit to Jerusalem for the festival of Passover (Pesach). Thousands of Jewish people from all over the Roman Empire made the same journey. While Jesus was a child he stayed at home, but when he was 12 years old he was allowed to go to Jerusalem with his parents. In the Jewish faith, children are thought to be grown up when they reach the age of 12. At the end of the Passover festival, Mary and Joseph set off home with all their friends and relations. They thought that Jesus was with their party but they soon found out that he had been left behind. They quickly returned to Jerusalem, but it took them three days to find him.

They found him in the Temple. He was talking and arguing with the religious leaders. His parents began to tell him off because they had been very worried about him. Jesus told them that he had come to earth to do what God wanted and he had to get on with his job. His parents did not really understand him but they took him back home. We do not hear anything else about Jesus for eighteen years.

DISCUSSION POINTS

1 *The Bible story of Jesus in the Temple.* You can use any additional information you need.

2 *The ways in which Jesus seemed to be the same as us.* In what ways was he different?

3 *The experience of being lost.* Encourage children to relate personal experiences, e.g. of fear, of being found, of the feelings of parents. How might Mary and Joseph have felt?

See Factsheets 3, 6 and 19, pages 12, 15 and 28.

COPYMASTER 5 NAME..

What happened where?

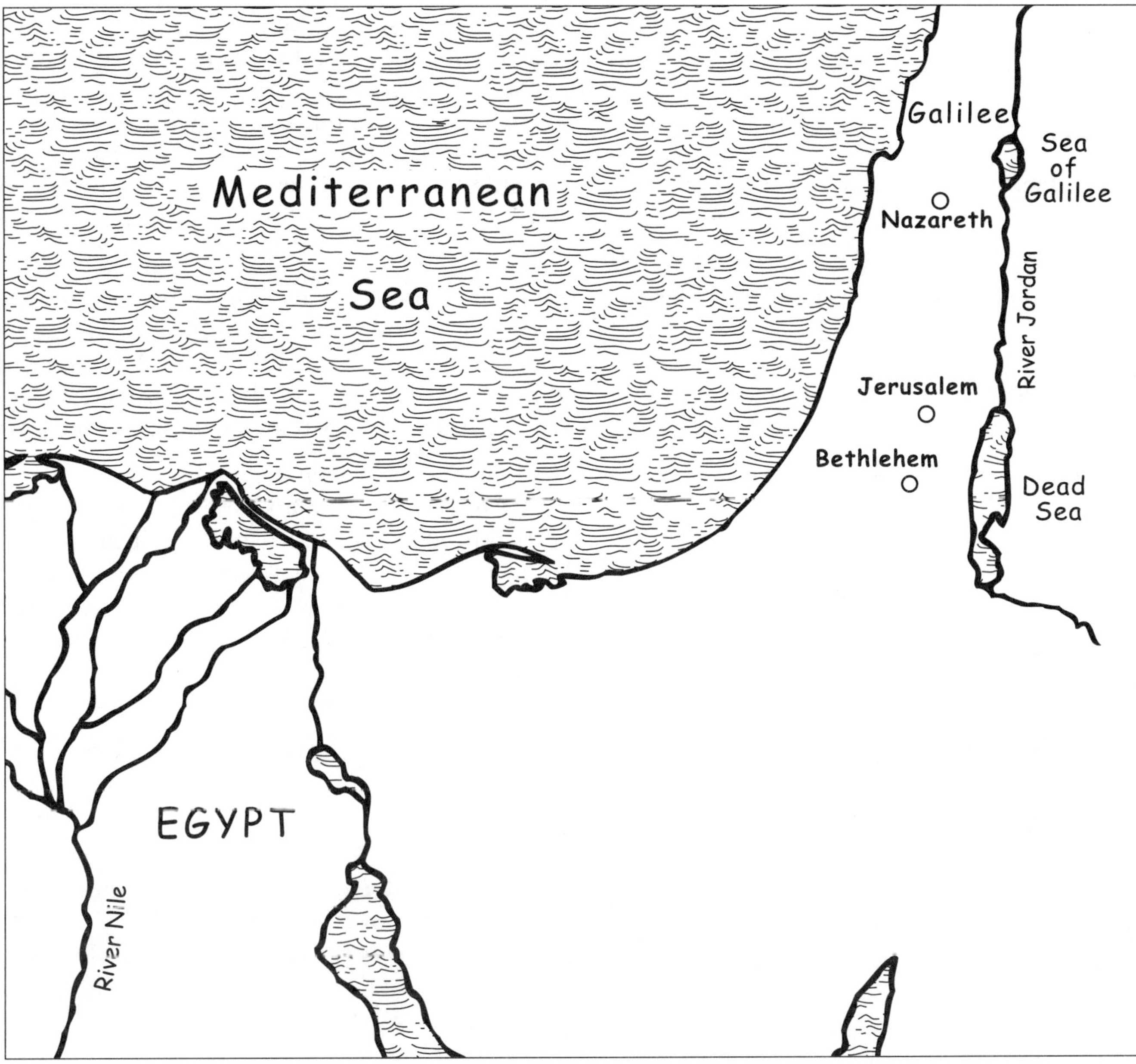

This map shows four places at which important events in the early life of Jesus took place. You can read about these events in these places in the Four Gospels:

a Matthew 2.1-12
b Matthew 2.13,14
c Matthew 2.19-23
d Luke 2.1-7.

1. Find each of these places in your Four Gospels and read about them.

2. Find the place where each event happened on the map.

3. Draw a picture to show each event.

Jesus is baptized

AIMS

The aims of this section are to introduce:

1 The preaching and baptism of John the Baptist

2 The baptism of Jesus

3 The confirmation which God gave to Jesus after his baptism

4 The Holy Spirit

5 The Christian practice of baptism.

Matthew 3.13-17; Mark 1.9-11; Luke 3.21-22

1 During the time that John was baptizing people in the River Jordan, Jesus came to him seeking to be baptized. Only Matthew saw the irony in this. Jesus, the sinless Son of God, was seeking a baptism which involved the forgiveness of sins. John wanted Jesus to baptize him but Jesus himself never baptized anyone. John hesitated and questioned the baptism but Jesus gave him an answer (Matthew 3.14,15) which suggests that it was God's will that Jesus should be baptized and so John went ahead.

2 As Jesus came up out of the water he alone saw heaven open up and the Spirit of God, in the form of a dove, come down and sit on his shoulder. Ever since the Spirit of God was said to have been 'brooding' over the waters of chaos before creation began in Genesis 1, the dove was used as a symbol of the Spirit.

3 Everyone, it seems, heard the voice speaking from heaven. It testified that God had broken his silence and was speaking again to the human race to state that Jesus was his Son. This was a theme that all of the Gospel writers were to develop in their accounts.

KEY WORDS

Baptism	John the Baptist
Heaven	Son of God
Holy Spirit	

THE STORY

John the Baptist came by his name because he baptized many people in the River Jordan. People came to him to be baptized because they wanted God to take away their sins. As he lowered them beneath the water John told them that their sins were forgiven. One day, Jesus came to John and asked to be baptized like everyone else. John was very surprised to see Jesus because John knew that Jesus was the Son of God, and didn't have any sins to be forgiven. Jesus replied that he wanted to be treated like everyone else and that this was God's will. So John baptized him.

As Jesus came out of the water he saw heaven open up above him. He saw God's Spirit coming down from heaven and sitting on his shoulder like a dove. Jesus was the only person who saw this. The other people heard God speak to Jesus. God announced that Jesus was his Son. He loved Jesus very much.

DISCUSSION POINTS

1 *The Bible story of the baptism of Jesus.*

2 *Baptismal services.* Children can bring their own baptismal certificates along or talk about a baptismal service that they have attended.

3 *The importance of washing.* The importance of this both physically and spiritually.

4 *The things that people do wrong.* How can they be forgiven? Who can forgive them? Why is forgiveness important?

See Factsheet 2, page 11.

 NAME...

John baptizes Jesus

Read Matthew 3.13-17.
Fill in the gaps in the sentences beneath each drawing.

John ____________ people in the River Jordan. He told them that they must be sorry for their __________ .

_______________ was surprised when _______________ came to him to be baptized.

The _________ _________ came in the form of a ___________ and sat on the ___________ of __________ .

Everyone heard the ___________ from ___________ saying that ________ was ___________ ___________ .

Jesus is tempted

AIMS

The aims of this section are to introduce:

1 The story of the temptations of Jesus

2 The Devil as a source of temptation

3 The rejection of the temptations by Jesus.

KEY WORDS

Angel	Mark
Devil	Matthew
Fasting	Son of God
Jerusalem	Temple
Luke	

Matthew 4.1-11; Luke 4.1-12

Both Matthew and Luke cover the temptations of Jesus in some detail although they place them in a different order. Mark only mentions them in passing. They all agree, however, that the temptations followed directly after the baptism of Jesus and were a prelude to the ministry of Jesus.

1 The first temptation happened after Jesus had fasted for forty days in the wilderness. He was tempted to turn the stones that lay around into loaves of bread to eat. Jesus meets this, as he does the other temptations, with a direct quotation from the Jewish Scriptures (Deuteronomy 6.14; 8.3 and Psalm 91.11-12).

2 The second temptation placed Jesus on the corner of the Great Temple Wall in Jerusalem which is more than 100 metres above the Kidron valley. In this temptation the Devil reminds Jesus that the Scriptures assure him that the angels will keep him safe whatever he does.

3 Jesus is tempted for the third time when the Devil offers him all the kingdoms of the world.

Most people conclude that these are not temptations in the literal sense, with a literal Devil. To think in this way is to miss the real point of the temptations. These temptations, and their source, are psychological and internal.

THE STORY

Jesus once lived in the desert for forty days and nights without having anything to eat. That must have been very difficult. After forty days and nights without food he was very hungry indeed. When he was feeling particularly hungry he heard a voice speaking to him.

"If you are God's Son, turn these stones into bread so that you won't be hungry any more." Jesus refused to do so because he knew that it was wrong to use God's power just for himself.

Then Jesus imagined that he was standing on top of the Temple, a long way off the ground. The voice spoke again.

"Throw yourself off," it said. "God will keep you safe and you will be King."

Jesus refused again. The voice did not give up. Jesus imagined that he was at the top of a very high mountain. He saw all the kingdoms of the world in front of his mind's eye. The voice told him that he could have them all if he would worship him. Jesus refused a third time. The voice gave up and left Jesus in peace for a time. God sent angels to Jesus to look after him and feed him.

DISCUSSION POINTS

1 *The Bible story of the temptations of Jesus.*

2 *Temptations in the lives of the children.* Talk about why people lie, cheat, steal, etc.

3 *The way in which temptation seems to come (the voice within).* Relate children's experiences of temptation to the temptations of Jesus.

4 *The voice.* Who do you think the voice was? Encourage children to understand that the voice was inside Jesus, and was his own voice. His struggle was with himself.

 NAME...

Being tempted

Each of these drawings shows someone being tempted to do wrong. Talk about each of the drawings with other people in your class and with your teacher.

1. Do you think that it would be wrong in each case to give in to the temptation?
2. Why do you think that it would be wrong?

Cheating

Taking, not sharing

Hurting and bullying

Envying

Jesus chooses his first disciples

AIMS

The aims of this section are to introduce:

1 The call of Jesus to Simon Peter, Andrew, Nathaniel and Matthew to be disciples

2 The different backgrounds from which these disciples came

3 What being a disciple of Jesus involved.

KEY WORDS

Ascension	Matthew
Disciple	Nazareth
Gospel	New
Heaven	Testament
John the Baptist	Peter
Levi	Rabbi

Matthew 9.9-13; John 1.35-42; 1.43-45

1 After introducing John the Baptist at the start of his Gospel, John describes how two fishermen, Simon Peter and Andrew, became disciples of Jesus through John's influence. Jesus immediately changed Simon's name to 'Cephas' (Peter) which means 'a rock'. Peter was the unquestioned leader of the twelve disciples and, after the ascension of Jesus into heaven, the first leader of the Early Church.

2 Jesus took the initiative in inviting Philip to become a disciple. This was unusual behaviour for a rabbi (teacher) since disciples usually attached themselves to a particular teacher. Philip was so impressed by Jesus that he persuaded Nathaniel to join them. Nathaniel was surprised that anyone of importance should come out of Nazareth which was an insignificant town.

3 Later in his ministry Jesus chose Matthew. This was a controversial choice since Matthew followed one of the most hated of all professions in Palestine – he was a tax-collector. Tax-collectors worked for the Romans and made their money by charging the Jewish communities over and above the tax demanded by the occupying army. (Matthew is probably the same person as 'Levi' in the list of the twelve disciples.) Almost certainly it was Matthew who wrote the first of the four Gospels in the New Testament.

THE STORY

Jesus wanted some close friends to travel with him and learn from him. Not only did he need them as friends but he also wanted to train them. They would continue his work after he left the earth. He was first approached by Simon who soon told his brother, Andrew, about Jesus. Both Simon and Andrew were fishermen but they left their boats behind when they became disciples. Jesus changed Simon's name to 'Peter' which means 'a rock'. Peter crops up time and time again in the Gospel stories.

Jesus was walking alongside the lake in Galilee when he saw Philip and asked him to become a follower. The first thing that Philip did was to tell his friend, Nathaniel, about Jesus. Nathaniel was more doubtful to begin with, because he didn't like anyone who came from Nazareth. But before long he too became a disciple.

It was a little while later that Jesus approached Matthew and invited him to become a disciple. Matthew was a very unpopular man because he was a tax-collector. He collected money for the Romans. After Jesus spoke to him Matthew threw a great feast. Some people wanted to know what Jesus was doing eating with people like Matthew. Jesus told them that God had sent him to help people just like Matthew.

DISCUSSION POINTS

1 *The decisions of Simon Peter, Andrew, Philip, Nathaniel and Matthew to become disciples of Jesus.*

2 *The decision to give up everything to follow Jesus.* What was involved in this decision? What did it mean to be a disciple? What might it mean to be a disciple of Jesus today?

3 *The choice of disciples.* Why did Jesus choose such a mixed bunch to become his closest friends?

See Factsheet 15, page 24.

 NAME..

Who is who?

The names of four of the disciples of Jesus are below. Follow the trail leading to each of their names. When you have found them write down one thing about each one.

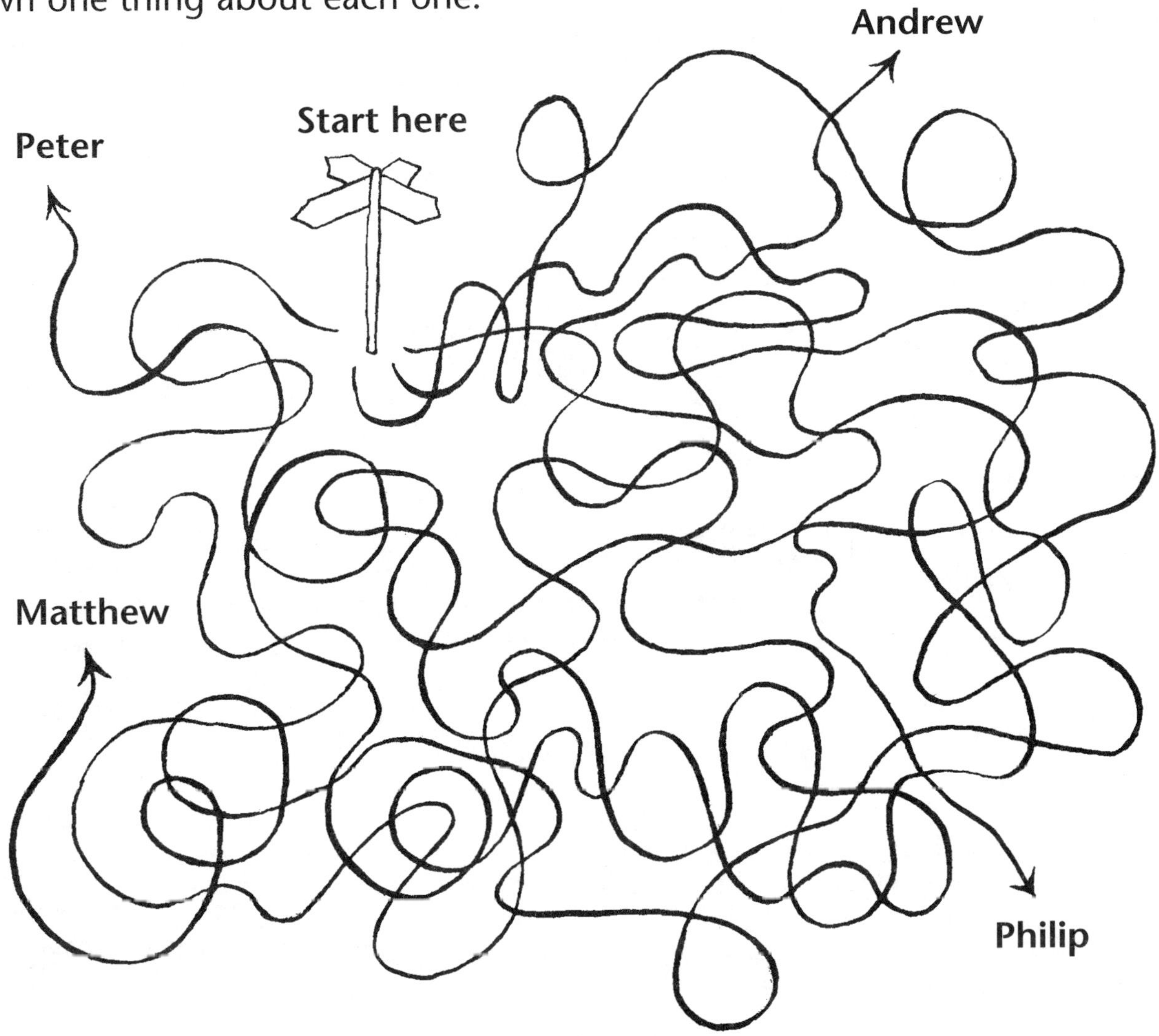

1. ______________________________

2. ______________________________

3. ______________________________

4. ______________________________

The twelve disciples

AIMS

The aims of this section are to introduce:

1 What it means to be a disciple

2 How Jesus chose his disciples

3 The twelve disciples.

KEY WORDS

Disciple	Mark
Gospel	Matthew
James	Peter
John	Thomas
Judas Iscariot	Zealot

Matthew 10.1-4; Mark 3.13-19; Luke 6.12-16

1 Mark, in his Gospel, places the choosing of the twelve disciples by Jesus immediately after his temptation. Perhaps that was intended to be significant. Maybe Mark wished to imply that the temptations brought home to Jesus his need for the help and support of others.

2 The number 12 is very significant in the Gospels. There were 12 tribes that made up the nation of Israel. After the original Israel rejected its Messiah, the 12 disciples form the basis for the 'new Israel', the Church. The 12 are chosen to fulfill two functions:

• to be in close touch with Jesus – to live with him, travel with him, talk to him and learn from him

• to go out and preach the Gospel (the Good News), to drive out demons and anoint the sick to heal them.

3 Jesus made more than one unexpected choice when selecting his disciples. Judas Iscariot (the 'dagger carrier') and Simon (not Peter) were Zealots. The Zealots were a fanatical group dedicated to the armed expulsion of the Romans from Palestine. Judas and Simon may seem to have been strange choices. So, too, was Matthew who was probably a tax-collector or a customs-officer on the toll-road which ran from Capernaum to the coast.

THE STORY

Jesus gathered together many men and women. These people followed him all over the place. They saw the miracles he performed and listened carefully to his teaching. But Jesus wanted to choose 12 special friends who would share his life intimately. One day, Jesus went up a hill and called to him the 12 men he wanted as followers. He told them they had been chosen to do some special work. He was going to send them out to preach about God.

They were a pretty mixed bunch of people. Their names were Simon Peter, Andrew, Philip, Nathaniel and Matthew. Then there were two brothers, James and John, who had such bad tempers that they were called 'the sons of thunder'. Another two disciples, Judas Iscariot and Simon, were Zealots. The Zealots carried a dagger under their cloak in case they had the chance to kill a Roman soldier. Much later it would be Judas who would betray Jesus to the Roman authorities. There were also a few disciples that we hear hardly anything about. Their names were Batholomew, another James, and Thaddaeus. Finally, there was Thomas whom we will meet again.

DISCUSSION POINTS

1 *The Bible account of the choosing of the 12 disciples.*

2 *Friendship.* Why do we need friends? What would we do if we didn't have them? What did Jesus look for in his friends?

3 *Odd choices of friends.* What makes us choose the friends we do? Why do others choose us to be their friends?

See Factsheet 5, page 14.

 NAME..

My close friends

Draw pictures of your two best friends above.

Why are they your best friends?

What do you like about them?

My close friends and I spend a lot of time together because:

1.

2.

3.

4.

5.

Jesus sends out his disciples

AIMS

The aims of this section are to introduce:

1 Those whom the disciples were sent out to reach (Jewish people)

2 The role the disciples were given (healing the sick, bringing the dead back to life, healing those suffering from leprosy and driving out demons)

3 The way that the disciples were expected to travel (without money or extra clothes)

4 The response of the disciples to those they met.

KEY WORDS

Disciples	Israel
Galilee	Jew
Gentile	

Matthew 10.5-15; Mark 6.7-13; Luke 9.1-6

1 Directly after choosing his 12 disciples, Jesus sent them out on a preaching and teaching mission. He told them not to take the road that led to the Gentiles (non-Jews) in the north, the Decapolis in the east or Samaria in the south. Instead they were to remain in Galilee to minister to the people of Israel (the Jews).

2 The message taken out by the disciples could be summed up in the words "The Kingdom of heaven is near" (Matthew 10.7). This was shown by the power of the disciples to perform miracles. Nobody was to be charged for receiving the message. The disciples were not to beg. They were to travel without the added encumbrances of extra clothes, shoes or walking stick.

3 As the disciples entered a house they were to give it their 'greeting'. If the people in the house did not welcome them they were to move on. Those who received the disciples received Jesus.

THE STORY

As soon as Jesus had chosen his 12 disciples he gave them a job to do. He sent them out into the villages and towns of nearby Galilee. He asked them to behave just as he would have done. They were to heal and help those in need. They would not be paid any wages for doing this. They were not to carry any money in their pockets or even a spare pair of sandals or an extra walking-stick. Nor were they to beg. But if people gave them food or money, they were to take it.

They were to depend on people to give them shelter at night. If they were welcomed into a house they could stay there. Jewish people always welcomed a traveller in to stay with them. If the house did not welcome them, however, they were to go elsewhere. Just as Jesus was a man in a hurry so were his disciples. They had a special message to carry and did not have any time to spare.

DISCUSSION POINTS

1 *The Bible story of Jesus sending out his disciples.*

2 *The work that Jesus had come to do.* Discuss the work given to the disciples and their role as ambassadors or representatives of Jesus.

3 *The disciples were sent out without any money or spare clothes.* Why?

 NAME...

Out on the job

Jesus sent his twelve disciples into nearby villages and towns. He gave them some clear instructions. You can find out what they were by reading Matthew 10.5-14.

The disciples were told to:

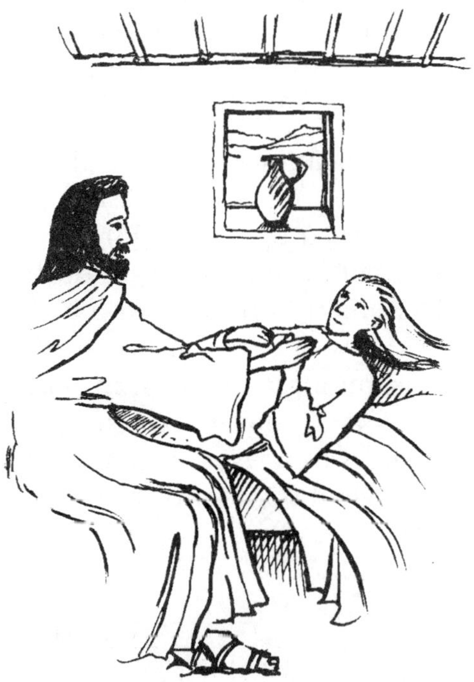

They were told not to:

When they arrived in a town or village Jesus told them to:

Peter's great confession

AIMS

The aims of this section are to introduce:

1 Peter as the spokesman for the disciples

2 The misunderstanding of the people about Jesus

3 The moment of inspiration when Peter identified Jesus as the Messiah.

Matthew 16.13-20; Mark 8.27-30; Luke 9.18-21

1 Usually the disciples are presented in the Gospels as failing to understand just what Jesus was about. Occasionally, however, the truth dawned on them. This incident at Caesarea Philippi is often described as a 'watershed' in the ministry of Jesus. Caesarea Philippi was a small town at the base of Mount Hermon.

2 The people varied in their opinions about Jesus. Some thought that he was John the Baptist brought back to life. To others he was Elijah, a very important Jewish prophet. There was a tradition that Elijah would return to earth before the Messiah appeared. Still others thought that he was Jeremiah, another important Jewish prophet. Nobody, it seems, thought that he was the Messiah. This was the leader that the Jews had expected for centuries to deliver them from their enemies. Jesus knew himself to be the Messiah but a suffering rather than a victorious, war-like figure. This was why he was reluctant to openly accept the title.

KEY WORDS

Disciple	Palestine
Elijah	Peter
Gospel	Pope
Jeremiah	Prophet
John the Baptist	Roman Catholic Church
Messiah	

3 Peter's identification of Jesus as the Messiah came out of the blue. Jesus used Peter's name (meaning 'the rock') to make a statement about the foundation of the Church. To Roman Catholics, who believe that Peter became the first Bishop of Rome (Pope) this is amongst the most important of all statements in the Gospels. Jesus gave to Peter the keys to heaven and hell. He then ordered the disciples not to tell anyone that he was the Messiah.

THE STORY

All of the disciples were Jewish. Palestine, the land which belonged to Jewish people, had been occupied by the Roman army for a long time. The Romans made life very hard for Jewish people. The Jews looked to God to send them a leader who would drive the Romans out of their country. This leader was called the Messiah. One day Jesus arrived in Caesarea Philippi with his disciples. He asked his disciples, "Who do the people think I am?". They told him that some people thought he was John the Baptist, even though King Herod had put John the Baptist to death. Others said that he was one of the old Jewish prophets, such as Elijah or Jeremiah, sent back to earth.

Jesus then turned to his disciples and asked them, "And who do you think I am?". The leader of the disciples by this time was Peter. He spoke for all of them. "We think that you are the Messiah," he told Jesus. In one way he was right. But they still had a lot to learn about Jesus. Jesus was not going to throw the Romans out of Palestine. Instead he was going to suffer and die. Nobody expected that to happen to the Messiah.

DISCUSSION POINTS

1 *The Bible story of Peter's great confession.*

2 *Children can put themselves in the place of those who came to listen to Jesus.* What would they have made of Jesus and what he said?

3 *Sudden moments of inspiration.* Where do these come from? Where did Peter's idea come from?

See Factsheets 1 and 4, pages 10 and 13.

 NAME..

What did they say?

Read Matthew 16.13-20.

Write down who answered Jesus's questions and what they said.

"Who do the people say that I am?"

____

"Who do you say that I am?"

____

Complete the following.

"Good for you, Simon, son of John, for ...

____

____

______________________ *"*

Who said this?

____

The Transfiguration

AIMS

The aims of this section are to introduce:

1 The small group of disciples (Peter, James and John) that Jesus shared his closest moments with

2 The Jewish festival of Sukkoth

3 The Transfiguration as another occasion for God to confirm that Jesus was his Son.

KEY WORDS

Baptism	Old Testament
Disciple	Peter
Elijah	Prophet
James	Sukkoth
John	Tabernacles
Moses	

Matthew 17.1-13; Mark 9.2-13; Luke 9.28-36

1 The story of the Transfiguration is clearly important for its contribution to our understanding of the way in which Jesus saw himself. In the story, Moses and Elijah, two of the most important figures in Jewish history, meet with Jesus and the three of them are transfigured. (This happened in the Old Testament when men 'met with God' and the obvious implication here is that is what happened.) It is useful to think of this event as a vision rather than a physical event.

2 Peter, sensing something of the greatness of the occasion, suggested building three tabernacles (huts) for Jesus, Moses and Elijah. This suggests that the event occurred during the Jewish festival of Tabernacles. For this festival, Jewish people built temporary shelters, and lived in them, to remind themselves of the huts that the Israelites lived in when they were in the wilderness. The building of such tabernacles is still an important part of the Jewish festival of Tabernacles (Sukkoth) which is celebrated each year.

3 The cloud that appeared in the story crops up often in the Bible as a symbol of the presence of God. The voice that spoke out of the cloud, saying "This is my own dear Son, with whom I am pleased. Listen to him!" has already been heard in Matthew 3.17. The whole vision terrified the disciples but almost immediately the vision ended.

THE STORY

A vision is something that a person sees in their mind. There are many visions in the Bible. One of them took place when Jesus spent some time on a mountain with Peter, James and John, his closest friends. In their vision (or dream) Peter, James and John noticed that the face, and clothes, of Jesus were shining white. They also saw that two great prophets from the Bible, Moses and Elijah, were talking to Jesus. Peter thought that it would be a good idea to build huts for Jesus, Moses and Elijah. The moment he suggested it the vision disappeared. It probably only lasted for a split second anyway, rather like a thought that flashes across your mind and then is lost.

The vision left the three disciples rather shaky. They wondered what it could have been about. But Jesus put his hands on their shoulders and told them not to worry. They realised that they had only seen Moses and Elijah in their minds. Together they began to climb down the mountain with Jesus. Jesus didn't want anyone else to know about what had happened. He told his disciples not to say a word to anyone.

DISCUSSION POINTS

1 *Pictures that children see in their minds.* Talk about dreams and day-dreaming. How real are they?

2 *What does it mean to call children the sons or daughters of their parents?* Was Jesus God's Son in the same way? If not, how was he God's Son?

3 *The friendship between Jesus and his three closest friends.* What might Jesus have expected from his friends? What do we expect of our best friends?

 NAME...

The vision

Read Matthew 17.1-13.

If you had seen this vision what would have frightened you most?

What did the voice from heaven say?

What did Jesus tell his disciples as they came down from the mountain?

When did a voice also say the same words?

Zacchaeus, the tax-collector

AIMS

The aims of this section are to introduce:

1 The story of Zacchaeus, one of the outsiders in Luke's Gospel

2 The welcome given by Jesus to those people who were hated by others

3 The cost to Zacchaeus of becoming a follower (giving away half of his wealth).

KEY WORDS

Gospel

Jericho

Luke

Palestine

Luke 19.1-10

1 The message of Jesus had universal appeal. Zacchaeus was not only a tax-collector, and therefore disliked by the local community, but he had the additional disadvantage of being very small! This meant that he had to climb a sycamore tree in order to see Jesus. (The idea of people having to overcome practical problems before finding help from Jesus is a common one in the Gospels.)

2 The wealthy had to give away their wealth before they could become followers. This was even more important when the wealth in question was gained in an immoral way. Luke makes this point at the start of his account and provides the solution at the end.

3 Jesus was willing to be entertained at the home of someone who was a social outcast. This became a major cause of disagreement between Jesus and the religious authorities. For them, eating with an outcast made a person ritually unclean themselves. Religious leaders went to great lengths not to come into contact with those considered to be unclean.

4 The importance of final salvation. Jesus was welcomed by Zacchaeus into his house. Zacchaeus said that he would give away a substantial part of his wealth. Jesus declared, "Salvation has come to his house today...". As so often in a Gospel account, Jesus uses the story as a metaphor. One of the most important teachings of Jesus says, "The Son of Man (Jesus) came to seek and save the lost." (Luke 19.10).

THE STORY

One day, Jesus was passing through a city called Jericho, in Palestine. By now he attracted large crowds of people wherever he went. This day was no exception. Everyone in the city came out to see him. One man in Jericho, Zacchaeus, was so small he couldn't see anything over the crowd. Zacchaeus was just about the most unpopular person in the city. He was a tax-collector and worked for the Romans. To see Jesus, Zacchaeus climbed up a sycamore tree. He was amazed when Jesus stopped beneath his tree and said that he must go to his home for a meal. The people were equally amazed. Didn't Jesus know what kind of man Zacchaeus was?

Zacchaeus was very excited. Other people who were with Jesus started to grumble. Surely Jesus must know what kind of person Zacchaeus was? Zacchaeus soon told Jesus what he intended to do. He would give away half of his money to the poor and if he had cheated anyone he would pay them back four times! Jesus thought that this was a wonderful offer. He told Zacchaeus that he, Zacchaeus, and his family had been saved that day.

DISCUSSION POINTS

1 *The Bible story of Zacchaeus meeting Jesus.*

2 *The atmosphere in Jericho when Jesus visited.* Why were the people so excited? What were the particular problems Zacchaeus had?

3 *The feelings of Zacchaeus when Jesus singled him out from the crowd.* What may have led to his offer to put everything right?

 NAME..

The story of Zacchaeus

Complete the sentences using the words below.

1. *The people ____________ because Jesus was eating with Zacchaeus.*

2. *Zacchaeus climbed up into a ______________ tree to see Jesus.*

3. *Jesus was travelling through the city of _____________ .*

4. *Zacchaeus told Jesus that he would give away some of his ___________ .*

5. *______________ was a ____________________ .*

6. *_____________ looked up and saw Zacchaeus in the tree.*

7. *Jesus told Zacchaeus that he wanted a __________ at his house.*

8. *Jesus told Zacchaeus that ______________ had come to his house.*

Jericho	grumbled	meal	riches	Zacchaeus
sycamore	tax-collector	Jesus	salvation	

Now cut out the sentences and put them in the right order to tell the story of Zacchaeus.

___

___

___

___

___

___

___

___

The rich, young ruler

AIMS

The aims of this section are to introduce:

1 The attitude of Jesus towards the Ten Commandments

2 The way that Jesus treated a sincere person who happened to be very rich

3 The reaction of the disciples to the words of Jesus.

KEY WORDS

Disciple

Jerusalem

Ten Commandments

Mark 10.17-31

This story, and its aftermath, falls conveniently into three sections:

1 Jesus encountered a rich man. Jesus was travelling to Jerusalem when a young man fell on his knees and addressed Jesus, reverently, as 'good teacher'. The man's subsequent question showed his seriousness. He asked, "What must I do to receive eternal life?". Jesus answered him by reminding him of six of the Ten Commandments and the man claimed to have kept them all. Jesus did not dispute this claim. Looking him straight in the face, Jesus then told the man that he only lacked one thing. He must go and sell all of his riches. When the man went away sadly, Jesus told his disciples, "How hard it will be for rich people to enter the Kingdom of God.".

2 This statement amazed the disciples. They wondered just who could enter God's Kingdom. In Mark 10.25 and 10.27 there are two of the most striking of all the comments of Jesus. People at that time believed that riches were a sign of God's blessing and so the words of Jesus were particularly difficult for them to understand.

3 Peter then claimed that the disciples had left everything to follow Jesus. His comment does not seem to follow on from what Jesus said. Jesus reminded him that those who have left everything will be rewarded many times over, both in this time and in the one to come.

THE STORY

You would really think that those people who are very rich would also be very happy. One person who was rich and unhappy came to Jesus one day. He wanted to know what he could do to make sure that he reached heaven. Jesus reminded him of the Ten Commandments – about loving God and loving each other. The man said that he had kept them all since he was a young lad. Jesus obviously liked him a lot because he said that only one thing might stop him reaching heaven – his money.

This really upset the man. It also upset the disciples of Jesus who were listening. Everyone thought that if you were rich it showed that God was blessing you. Now Jesus was saying just the opposite. The rich man went away very sad and the disciples of Jesus were amazed by what Jesus had said. Jesus gave them something to think about. He told them that it was easier for a camel to go through the eye of a needle than for a rich man to enter heaven. That left everyone very confused.

DISCUSSION POINTS

1 *The Bible story of the rich man who came to Jesus.*

2 *The Ten Commandments.* How many of them do you know? Go through one or two of them, explaining what they mean. Look at those that have particular relevance to the children – do not steal, honour your father and mother, etc.

3 *Riches.* Put this into the modern context of someone who wins a lot of money on the National Lottery. Is it always a good thing? How would you respond if it was you? Would you be very happy? Would you stay happy?

 NAME..

Winning the Lottery

It is your lucky night. You guess all six balls correctly.
You win just over £2,000,000.

Write down four things you would do with the money.

1. ______________________________

____

____

____

2. ______________________________

____

____

____

3. ______________________________

____

____

____

4. ______________________________

____

____

____

Now imagine that Jesus is on earth today. You bump into him on the street and tell him that you have just won the £2,000,000.

What do you think he might tell you to do?

____

____

____

____

____

Holy Week

AIMS

The aims of this section are to introduce:

1 The events which led up to the death and resurrection of Jesus (these will be dealt with individually in subsequent sections)

2 The contrast between what happened to Jesus when he triumphantly entered the city of Jerusalem and what happened a few days later

3 The links between the events in the life of Jesus and special days which are celebrated by the Christian Church.

KEY WORDS

Disciple	Judas Iscariot
Easter Sunday	Last Supper
Good Friday	Maundy Thursday
Holy Week	Palm Sunday
Jerusalem	Sunday

Easter is the most important time of the year for all Christians. It celebrates the events in the life of Jesus which led to his death and resurrection. The final week of his life is celebrated as 'Holy Week'. This begins on Palm Sunday when Jesus entered the city of Jerusalem on a donkey. It ends on Easter Sunday.

1 *Palm Sunday.* On this day Jesus entered Jerusalem as his disciples, and the crowd, spread palm branches and their cloaks on the road in front of him. Many churches hold processions on this day which are often led by a small child riding a donkey. We will look at Palm Sunday in detail on pages 60 and 61.

2 *Maundy Thursday.* On this day Christians remember the Last Supper that Jesus ate with his disciples (see pages 68 and 69) as well as the occasion of Jesus washing the feet of his disciples (see pages 70 and 71).

3 *Good Friday.* This is the most serious day in the Christian Year when the death of Jesus at Calvary is remembered (see page 155).

4 *Easter Sunday.* This is the happiest day in the Christian Year when Christians, in many different ways, celebrate the rising of Jesus from the dead.

THE STORY

This is the most important story in the Christian faith. Jesus had made many enemies and they were looking for ways to end his life. The story began, however, on a note of excitement as Jesus entered the city of Jerusalem. He was riding a donkey and the people were spreading palm leaves and coats on the road in front of him. They were treating him like a king. This happened on a Sunday. Three days later Jesus knew that his life was soon going to end. He wanted to share a last meal with his disciples. At this meal he told them that one of them would betray him to the Romans. To help them remember him after he was dead, Jesus gave his disciples a special meal. As Jesus predicted, Judas Iscariot betrayed him and he was arrested and put to death on a cross. Christians today remember this each year on Good Friday.

They also remember what happened two days later on Easter Sunday. On this day, they believe, Jesus came back to life. After spending a little time with his disciples he left the earth for the last time.

DISCUSSION POINTS

1 *The events in the Bible which stretch from Palm Sunday to Easter Sunday.* Underline the importance of these events to Christians.

2 *A brainstorming session with the children.* Tell them that you want them to remember as much as they can about these events. This can be a written or a verbal exercise.

3 *The events of Holy Week and the link with children's experiences.* What can children recall of events during this week? Have they come across a Palm Sunday procession?

COPYMASTER 15 NAME..

Through Holy Week

There are four main days in Holy Week:

Good Friday — Maundy Thursday
Palm Sunday — Easter Sunday

Put these four days in the order in which they happen:

1. ______________________ *2.* ______________________

3. ______________________ *4.* ______________________

Here are four events that are celebrated on these days.
Which day is each event celebrated on?

Jesus entered Jerusalem on a donkey.
____

Jesus was put to death.
____

Jesus rose from the dead.
____

Jesus shared a meal with his disciples.
____

Can you find out one thing that Christians may do to celebrate each of these days:

Palm Sunday ______________________
____

Maundy Thursday ______________________
____

Good Friday ______________________
____

Easter Sunday ______________________
____

Jesus enters Jerusalem

AIMS

The aims of this section are to introduce:

1 The beginning of the last week in the life of Jesus

2 The idea of Jesus, God's Messiah, as a peace-making king.

KEY WORDS

David	Old Testament
Holy Week	Palestine
Jerusalem	Palm Sunday
Matthew	Passover
Messiah	Prophet
Moses	

Matthew 21.1-11

1 Palm Sunday begins the events of Holy Week as it was at this time that Jesus drew near to the city of Jerusalem. This city was the political and religious capital of Palestine. The Jewish prophets had encouraged the people to believe that God's Messiah would first show himself in Jerusalem.

2 Many pilgrims will have been in Jerusalem at this time to celebrate Passover, the most important Jewish festival. Passover commemorates the deliverance of the Jews, under the leadership of Moses, from slavery in Egypt.

3 Matthew describes Jesus entering Jerusalem riding "on a donkey and a colt, the foal of a donkey". This fulfilled an Old Testament prophecy. Zechariah (9.9-12) prophesied that the Messiah would come to Jerusalem in victory but also in humility. The donkey is a sign of humility. In direct contrast, a warrior king would enter the city on a horse. By fulfilling this prophecy Jesus was announcing to the people who he was.

4 Many Churches today celebrate Palm Sunday by holding a procession led by a donkey, often ridden by a small child.

THE STORY

Jesus was travelling towards the city of Jerusalem with his disciples. He wanted to celebrate the important Jewish festival of Passover with them. When they had almost reached the city Jesus stopped. He chose two of his disciples and asked them to collect a donkey from a nearby village. The disciples did as they were told and brought the donkey to Jesus. Some of the disciples put their coats on the donkey's back and Jesus climbed up and sat on an animal that had not been ridden before. He then rode towards the city of Jerusalem. Many people wanted to show that they were glad to see him. Some spread their coats on the road in front of him as a royal carpet for Jesus to ride on while others cut down palm branches and spread them out. As Jesus passed by they shouted out, "God bless Him who comes in the name of the Lord. Praise to David's son.". As Jesus looked round at the crowd he saw that everyone was joining in. He was just like a king arriving at his coronation.

DISCUSSION POINTS

1 *The Bible story of the entry of Jesus into Jerusalem.*

2 *Any procession that the children might have seen.* What was the occasion? Did many people watch it? Were they excited? If so, why?

3 *What it's like to be in a crowd.* How easy is it for a crowd to become excited about something (e.g. a football match, a pop concert, etc.)? Point out that the feeling soon passes. The same people welcoming Jesus here into Jerusalem were to be, within a few days, demanding his death.

See Factsheet 3, page 12.

 NAME..

Jesus is welcomed into Jerusalem

Read Matthew 21.1-11.

1. What can you see in the drawing?

____

____

____

____

____

____

2. Into which city did Jesus ride on a donkey?

____

____

____

3. Why did he ride on a donkey?

____

____

____

____

____

____

____

____

4. What did the disciples of Jesus and the people do?

____

____

____

____

____

____

____

5. What did the people shout out?

____

____

____

____

____

____

____

____

6. Imagine that you were in the crowd on that day. On a separate piece of paper, describe what you saw.

Jesus loses his temper

AIMS

The aims of this section are to introduce:

1 The surprising event of Jesus losing his temper

2 The reason why Jesus lost his temper (the exploitation of the poor and needy)

3 The welcome that the children gave to Jesus in the Temple.

KEY WORDS

Court of the Gentiles

John

Matthew

Messiah

Son of David

Temple

Matthew 21.12-17

Although John places his account of the cleansing of the Temple in Jerusalem much earlier in the ministry of Jesus (2.13-22) it fits much more happily at the beginning of the last week.

1 All sacrifices in the Temple had to be paid for in special Temple money. The money-changers converted the standard Greek and Roman currency into Temple currency and that was the problem. They charged a rate of interest which made them a considerable amount of money. Jesus drove them out of the Temple precincts.

2 The prophet Isaiah had looked forward to the time when the Temple would be called 'a house of prayer'. These fraudulent commercial activities, however, had turned the building into a 'den of thieves'. Matthew tells us that the blind and the crippled came to Jesus in the Temple. The only part of the Temple that such people were allowed to enter was the outer 'Court of the Gentiles'. Although they were not allowed any further, Jesus healed them. By his two actions, cleansing the Temple and healing those in need, Jesus was showing that he was in opposition to what the Temple then stood for.

3 These actions greatly annoyed the religious leaders but, as Matthew reports, the children recognised who Jesus was (the Son of David). When the leaders question him on this he quotes the Jewish Scriptures again to them (this time from Psalm 8.2).

THE STORY

This is rather a surprising story about Jesus. The most beautiful building in Jerusalem was the Temple. It was almost 400 metres around the outer wall. People came to the building to offer sacrifices (of animals or birds) to God. They had to pay for these sacrifices in special Temple money. They could only buy this money in the Temple itself. To change their money into the Temple money they used money-changers. The money-changers charged them a lot of money for this service. Jesus was very annoyed by this and went through the Temple with a whip, overturning the tables of the money-changers. As you can imagine, this made him many enemies.

It also made him many friends (especially amongst blind and disabled people). They were stopped from going very far into the Temple but they found Jesus in the outer court. He healed them. The religious leaders were very annoyed. They were even more annoyed when they heard little children calling Jesus the Messiah. When they complained to Jesus he told them that the Scriptures said that little children would give perfect praise to God.

DISCUSSION POINTS

1 *The Bible story of Jesus clearing the Temple and the implications of this.*

2 *What makes you angry?* Have you ever grown angry when you have seen other people being mistreated? What is 'righteous anger'?

3 *This is the only time that Jesus used physical force against others.* What made him particularly angry on this occasion? Encourage children to re-enact this scene through role play.

See Factsheets 3 and 6, pages 12 and 15.

 NAME..

How do you think they felt?

Read Matthew 21.12-17.
Put yourself in the shoes of the people below.

How do you think these people felt when Jesus cleansed the Temple?

The money-changers

The blind and disabled people

The religious leaders

The children who looked on

The widow's offering

AIMS

The aims of this section are to introduce:

1 The short, but very important, story of the widow putting her offering into the Temple treasury

2 Why Jesus saw her gift as being much more valuable than that of others

3 The example of the widow and what it teaches about the meaning of giving.

KEY WORDS

Court of the Gentiles	Luke
Court of the Women	Palestine
Disciple	Temple
Gentile	

Mark 12.41-44; Luke 21.1-4

Luke has told how the teachers of the Law victimised and exploited widows (Luke 20.45-47). This leads to a story of how one such widow set an example of true giving. There are two main points here:

1 The setting for this incident was the Court of the Women in the Temple. Only Gentiles were allowed to enter the outer court (the Court of the Gentiles) but both Jewish men and women were able to enter the Court of the Women. The Temple treasury was located in the Court of the Women. Jesus sat down on a bench from which he was able to watch the people put their offerings into one of thirteen trumpet-shaped boxes set aside for that purpose.

2 It was not the rich, with their large offerings, that caught the eye of Jesus but a poor widow who put in 'two little copper coins, worth a penny'. These were two of the smallest coins in circulation in Palestine. Jesus wanted his disciples to learn a very important lesson from what he had seen.

THE STORY

This story tells of what was only a very brief event in the life of Jesus. But the event had a very important meaning. One day, Jesus was sitting in the Court of the Women in the Temple. Both men and women were allowed into this part of the Temple. There were thirteen small boxes, shaped like trumpets, in this part of the holy building. People dropped their offerings for the Temple into one of the boxes. Jesus saw several rich people come up and drop large sums of money into a box. Often the rich people made sure that other people saw what they were giving. Jesus wasn't very impressed with them.

Then, he saw a poor, old widow shuffle up to one of the boxes. Somehow he managed to see what she was putting in. It was two small coins which together added up to just a penny. She would have given more but she simply didn't have the money. That didn't matter to Jesus. He called his disciples over to him. "I want you to understand," he said to them, "that this poor widow has given more than all the rich people put together. They could afford what they gave but the poor woman could not even afford two copper coins". She was the one who was given the approval of Jesus.

DISCUSSION POINTS

1 *The Bible story of the poor widow.* Allow children to draw their own lessons from this.

2 *The idea of giving money and wanting other people to know about it.* Why should someone do that? Why did Jesus criticise the action?

3 *The action of the widow and why Jesus found it more acceptable.* What was so valuable in what she did? How can this be applied to giving in many different ways?

See Factsheet 6, page 15.

 NAME..

A little means a lot

Read Mark 12.41-44.

What did Jesus say about the rich people who gave money?

What did Jesus say about the poor widow?

Why do you think Jesus was so pleased with the poor widow?

Jesus is anointed in Bethany

AIMS

The aims of this section are to introduce:

1 The reason for the inclusion of this story in the Gospels (it is a simple expression of a woman's love for Jesus)

2 The revelation of the character of Judas as a greedy thief.

KEY WORDS

John

Judas Iscariot

Mark

Matthew

Matthew 26.6-13; Mark 14.3-9; John 12.1-7

Only John refers to Mary by name as the woman who anointed Jesus whilst in Matthew and Mark she is anonymous. Only Matthew and Mark mention that the meal took place in the house of Simon, who had a 'dreaded skin disease'. Neither Matthew nor Mark mentions Lazarus. But all three accounts clearly refer to the same event. There are three main points to think about:

1 The action of Mary in anointing the feet of Jesus was an expression of love. Spices and ointments were very expensive because they had to be imported. Mary's offering was valued at one year's wages for an ordinary working person. Wiping the feet of Jesus with her hair was an act of complete dedication and reverence.

2 Judas Iscariot reappears in this story. Judas was the treasurer of the disciples and John emphasises that he used this position to make himself rich. He shows his financial interest by complaining that the ointment could have been sold and the money used to support the poor.

3 Jesus makes the point that Mary, by her action, has anticipated his impending death. Jesus replied, "Leave her alone! Let her keep what she has for the day of my burial. You will always have poor people with you, but you will not always have me." (John 12.7,8). This shows that Jesus knew he was facing death. It highlights the failure of the many attempts that Jesus made to educate his disciples into accepting that he was about to die.

THE STORY

Jesus had already visited Bethany. He had brought Lazarus back from the dead on a previous visit. Now he was back in the village and enjoying a meal which had been given in his honour. As he ate, Jesus, like all the guests, was leaning on one elbow with his legs out in front of him. Mary, the sister of Lazarus, was one of those serving the food but she had a surprise in store for everyone. She had brought a very expensive box of perfume with her. Suddenly, she broke the box open and began to spread it on the feet of Jesus with her hair. Everyone in the room could smell the ointment.

Judas Iscariot was there with the other disciples. He was very upset. He was the group's treasurer and said that the ointment should have been sold by Mary. She could then have given the money to the poor. But he was not really worried about the poor. He wanted to help himself to the money in the bag. Jesus, however, was very pleased at what Mary had done. She had shown how much she loved him.

DISCUSSION POINTS

1 *Things that make us grateful.* Who are we grateful to? What kinds of things make us grateful? How might we express our gratitude? Is it important to show that we are grateful to others?

2 *The relationship between gratitude and love.* How do we know that the woman in the story loved Jesus?

3 *Why was it important for this woman to show her love for Jesus?* Why is it important to help poor people?

 NAME..

Being grateful and showing it

Read John 12.1-7.

Why was Mary grateful to Jesus?

How did Mary show her love for Jesus?

Why was Judas upset?

What did Jesus say about Mary?

The Last Supper

AIMS

The aims of this section are to introduce:

1 The last meal that Jesus ate with his disciples

2 The betrayal of Jesus by Judas

3 The link between this last meal and the Christian service of Holy Communion.

KEY WORDS

Breaking of Bread	Eucharist	Lord's Supper
Disciple	Holy Communion	Mass
Divine	Liturgy	Passover

Mark 14.34-42

1 Jesus and his disciples were all Jewish and it was natural for them to celebrate the Passover meal together. Jesus took some bread, broke it into pieces, gave thanks to God and gave it to his disciples. He then poured out some wine and they all drank together.

2 The service of Holy Communion, a re-creation of this last meal, carries many different names in Christian worship: Eucharist or Holy Communion (Anglican); Mass (Roman Catholic); The Divine Liturgy (Orthodox) and the Lord's Supper or the Breaking of Bread (Nonconformist).

THE STORY

One evening, Jesus sat down with his disciples to eat a very special meal. It was called the Seder, or Passover, meal and was to remember a very important event in Jewish history – the exodus of Jewish people from slavery in Egypt. Jesus used the meal to tell his disciples something very important. He warned them that one of them would hand him over to the Roman soldiers who would put him to death. At this moment the disciple who was going to do this, Judas Iscariot, got up and walked out of the room. The disciples now knew who Jesus was talking about.

Jesus wanted his disciples to remember him, and his death, every time they had a meal together. He knew that they would eat bread and drink wine every day so this was a good way for them to remember what he had taught them. Soon after his death, other Christians also began to remember Jesus in this way. They ate a slice of bread and drank from a goblet of wine to remind themselves of his death. Christians still do this when they go to Church today. The Church service at which Christians do this has many different names. Often it is called 'Holy Communion' or the 'Eucharist'.

DISCUSSION POINTS

1 *The Bible story of the Last Supper.*

2 *Show photographs or talk about meals with which the children are familiar.* Why do families eat together? Who is invited? What kind of food is eaten?

3 *Meals in the time of Jesus.* How did people eat? In what order? What foods would they have eaten? What were the rules about eating together?

See Factsheet 12, page 21.

 NAME...

The last meal

Read Mark 14.34-42.

What is happening in the drawing above?

Write about:

1. Judas leaving the room

2. Jesus breaking the bread

3. Jesus pouring the wine.

Jesus washes the feet of his disciples

AIMS

The aims of this section are to introduce:

1 The story of Jesus washing the feet of his disciples

2 Jesus setting an example for others to follow (loving and serving others is at the heart of the Christian Gospel).

KEY WORDS

Disciple

Gospel

Judas

Peter

John 13.2-7

By the time that this event was about to take place, Judas had already shown his determination to betray Jesus. No motive, however, has been given for the actions of Judas and his determination was put down to satanic influence. His inner conflict has been viewed as being to do with rebellion against God.

1 John tells us that Jesus was aware that God had given everything to him. He knew that he was about to return to his Father in heaven. He wants his readers to understand the enormity of the humility that lay behind the action of Jesus in washing the feet of his disciples. He wants us to understand that Jesus was not an innocent victim of events that were out of his control.

2 Jesus and his disciples had come to the banquet room straight from the street. On such an occasion the host would normally call upon the most menial servant to wash the feet of his guests. But since this was a secret meeting, no servants were present. None of the disciples volunteered for the task since it would have involved an admission of inferiority to the others. So Jesus set about the task himself to teach the disciples a very important spiritual lesson.

3 The conversation between Jesus and Peter (verses 6-9) shows the particular character of Peter, which is apparent throughout the Gospels.

THE STORY

One evening, Jesus sat down with his disciples for a meal. It had been a very hot day and they were all tired and dusty. After they had finished their meal, Jesus poured some water into a bowl and began to wash the feet of his disciples. This was usually the job of the lowest servant in the family and the disciples were very surprised. Simon Peter, in particular, was upset and he asked Jesus what he was doing. Jesus told him that he could not be a disciple unless he allowed Jesus to do this. Simon Peter wanted to be a disciple above everything else and so he let Jesus continue.

After Jesus had finished he sat down again with his disciples. He wanted to find out if they had understood the meaning of what he had done. He had washed their feet to teach them a lesson. This lesson was that they must look after each other just as Jesus had looked after them.

DISCUSSION POINTS

1 *The Bible story and the lesson of humility.*

2 *How would you feel if someone very important began to wash your feet?* Would you be embarrassed? What would embarrass you the most?

 NAME...

Whose feet?

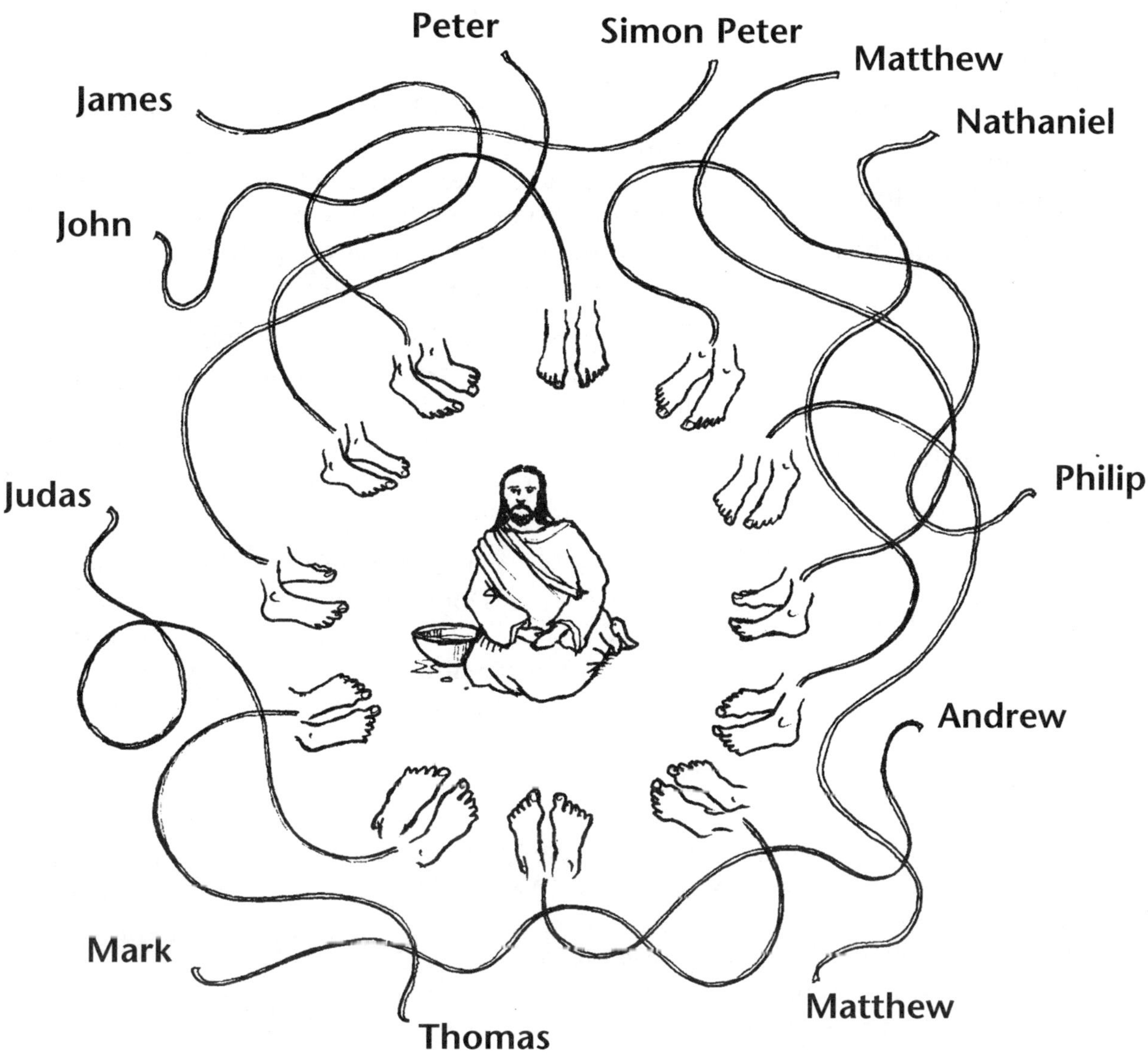

Find out whose feet Jesus is washing.

Why did Jesus wash the feet of his disciples?

____

____

____

____

____

Garden of Gethsemane

AIMS

The aims of this section are to introduce:

1 The inner group of disciples (Peter, James and John) who shared the most personal moments in the life of Jesus

2 The deep sorrow that Jesus felt at his approaching death

3 The weakness of the disciples.

KEY WORDS

Aramaic	Judas
Disciple	Mark
James	Peter
John	

Matthew 26.36-46; Mark 14.32-42; Luke 22.39-46

Gethsemane was a garden located on the lower slopes of the Mount of Olives. Jesus went there frequently to be alone or to be with his disciples. But on the occasion of his last visit there he faced a crucial test.

1 Jesus went with just three of his disciples (Peter, James and John). He must have felt the need for their presence at this time of crisis. Mark's Gospel expresses the deep agony that Jesus felt. Three times he left his disciples and withdrew to be alone with God. The disciples were supposed to watch out for the people Jesus knew would soon be arriving to arrest him.

2 The prayer of Jesus to God is introduced by the word 'Abba'. This is the familiar Aramaic word for 'Father'. Jewish people did not use this word to address God because they thought it was disrespectful. Jesus simply prayed that the 'cup of wrath' might be taken from him (i.e. his future suffering).

3 Each time that Jesus returned to his disciples he found them sleeping. Doubtless they were tired because the time was late but Jesus clearly expected them to be able to watch out for him for a while. Peter was singled out because of his boast that he was prepared to die for Jesus.

THE STORY

Jesus had just shared his last meal with his disciples. Now he took three of them (Peter, James and John) with him to the Garden of Gethsemane. He wanted them to keep a look out whilst he went a little way ahead of them to pray. (Jesus was in great danger at that time.) He told them that his sadness was such a great weight that he was almost crushed by it. Three times he went to pray only to return and find the disciples asleep, instead of keeping watch. The disciples were very embarrassed when Jesus woke them up because they had told him that they would never let him down.

The third time Jesus found Peter, James and John asleep, he looked up to see Judas coming with the Roman soldiers to arrest him. The disciples would have no chance to sleep now. Jesus warned his disciples that he was about to be arrested by sinful men. He then pointed out who was leading the soldiers. It was the same person, Judas Iscariot, that he had spoken about earlier. Can you remember when?

DISCUSSION POINTS

1 *The Bible story of Jesus in the Garden of Gethsemane.*

2 *Treachery.* What is treachery? Why would someone want to let their best friend down like this? Have we ever betrayed our friends?

3 *The struggle that Jesus had in the Garden of Gethsemane.* Was he afraid? What was he afraid of? Talk about Jesus as a human being. What side of Jesus comes out in this episode?

 NAME..

In the Garden of Gethsemane

Jesus was very sad as he went into the Garden of Gethsemane. He took Peter, James and John (three of his disciples) with him. He left them on their own and told them to pray for him. Jesus went a little way from them and prayed to God on his own. He came back to his disciples and found them asleep. He woke them up.

1. Was Jesus happy or sad as he went into the Garden of Gethsemane?

2. How many friends did Jesus take with him into the Garden of Gethsemane?

3. What were the names of the friends who went with him?

4. What did Jesus tell his friends to do?

5. What did Jesus do when he left his friends?

6. What were Jesus's friends doing when he came back?

7. What did Jesus do?

Jesus is arrested

AIMS

The aims of this section are to introduce:

1 The arrest of Jesus by the Temple guard

2 The kiss with which Judas betrayed Jesus (and the irony that a kiss is a sign of love)

3 The behaviour of the other disciples (a show of bravado and then a speedy departure).

KEY WORDS

Disciple	Mark
High Priest	Peter
Judas	Temple

Matthew 26.47-56; Mark 14.43-50; Luke 22.47-53; John 18.5-11

1 The arrest of Jesus marks the beginning of what Christians call 'the Passion of Christ'. After eating his last meal with his disciples Jesus foretold that they would all desert him. He then went to pray with them in Gethsemane and it was there that a group of Temple guards, led by Judas Iscariot, found him. They came armed with swords and clubs, apparently expecting trouble.

2 John tells us that it was Peter who tried to prevent the arrest of Jesus by cutting off the ear of the High Priest's servant. Jesus's rebuke to Peter and his restoration of the servant's ear are not recorded by Mark. It was the manner of the arrest that particularly upset Jesus. He was teaching every day in the outer court of the Temple and they could have arrested him there. His arrest was the fulfilment of a prophecy in the Jewish Scriptures (Isaiah 53.12). The disciples subsequently failed to stand by Jesus and deserted him.

THE STORY

Jesus was still talking to his disciples in the Garden of Gethsemane when a crowd of people arrived. They were led by Judas and included soldiers who were normally on duty in the Temple. Judas came up to kiss Jesus. Kissing someone usually shows that you are their friend. The disciples were upset when they realised what was about to happen. One of them, probably Peter, drew his sword and lunged towards the head of the High Priest's servant. He missed but sliced off the man's ear instead. Jesus told Peter to put his sword away. He then stretched out his hand and healed the ear immediately.

Jesus was very upset. He was upset at being arrested by a crowd carrying swords and clubs. He asked them why they hadn't arrested him in the Temple where he taught every day. They did not say so but there was a very good reason why they hadn't. The soldiers were worried at what might have happened if they had arrested Jesus in the middle of a large crowd of people. This, by the way, is almost the end of Judas. We are told that he was so upset by what he had done that he killed himself.

DISCUSSION POINTS

1 *The Bible story of the arrest of Jesus.*

2 *Loyalty and betrayal.* Discuss what it was that made Judas go through with his betrayal. Could he have stopped at the last minute?

3 *Who would you be loyal to?* Why would you be loyal to that particular person? What would it mean to betray that person?

The arrest

Complete the sentences using the words below.

Jesus took ______ of his disciples with him into the ______ of ______. Their names were ______, ______ and ______. Jesus told them to ______ with him but they fell ______. In the end Jesus saw ______ and some ______ coming to arrest him.

Garden pray soldiers three
Gethsemane Peter asleep
James Judas John

Match up the two halves of each sentence. Copy out the completed sentences below in the right order. The first one has been done for you.

Jesus went	*went with Jesus into the garden.*
Jesus prayed to	*cut off a man's ear.*
Jesus was	*stay awake.*
Peter	*into the Garden of Gethsemane.*
Peter, James and John	*Abba (Father).*
The disciples could not	*arrested by some soldiers.*

Jesus prayed to Abba (Father).

Jesus before the Sanhedrin

AIMS

The aims of this section are to introduce:

1 The first trial of Jesus (before the Jewish Council of the Sanhedrin)

2 The condemnation of Jesus by the Sanhedrin (for the religious crime of blasphemy)

3 The behaviour of Peter after Jesus had been arrested (he followed from a distance).

Matthew 26.57-68; Mark 14.53-65; Luke 22.54-55; 63-71; John 18.13-14; 19-24

1 The trial of Jesus took place in two stages. There was a religious trial followed by a civil one. The Sanhedrin was the Jewish Supreme Council composed of seventy religious leaders under the chairmanship of the High Priest. However, on this occasion Jesus was brought before Annas, the previous High Priest, before appearing in front of Caiaphas, the present holder of that office.

2 The meeting before Caiaphas (in an upstairs room of his palace) was the most important. Enough of the Sanhedrin were present to constitute a quorum. According to the Gospel writers many witnesses were produced who made damaging accusations against Jesus. But they could not agree amongst themselves. For the leader of the Supreme Council, however, the only charge that mattered came when Jesus admitted to being the Messiah (God's chosen leader who would deliver his people, the Jewish people, from their enemies). Up until now, Jesus had avoided making a direct claim to be the Messiah because people misunderstood what the Messiah had been sent to do.

KEY WORDS

Blasphemy	Messiah
Caiaphas	Palestine
Gospel	Peter
High Priest	Sanhedrin

3 The tearing of one's clothes was a sign of great grief. The High Priest of the Supreme Council here showed that he had just heard a blasphemous statement by tearing his clothes. Blasphemy was an affront to the majesty of God. All of the Sanhedrin agreed with their leader's judgement and pronounced that Jesus was worthy of death.

THE STORY

After Jesus was arrested he was taken to the palace of the High Priest, Caiaphas (a very important man in Palestine). Peter followed him at a distance, hoping that nobody would recognise him.

Meanwhile many people were accusing Jesus and trying to make out that he was a great threat to the Romans. Their stories, however, did not agree. Caiaphas stood up and asked Jesus, "Are you the Messiah that people say you are?" (Jewish people had been expecting the Messiah to come for a long time. They believed that he was going to lead the Jews into battle with the Romans.) Jesus was not going to lead anyone into battle but he replied, "I am the Messiah". At this, the High Priest expressed pain because he believed that Jesus had committed blasphemy. And blasphemy was a very great crime. The High Priest believed that he would have to punish Jesus. Then he did a strange thing. With his hands he tore his own clothes. In those days, people did that very occasionally when they were grieving the loss of a loved one. It showed that the pain was too much to bear.

DISCUSSION POINTS

1 *The Bible story of Jesus appearing before the Sanhedrin.*

2 *What might it feel like to be on trial for your life?* Why did Jesus 'not try very hard'?

 NAME...

Jesus on trial

Read Mark 14.53-65.

After Jesus was arrested he was taken to the house of the High Priest. Peter followed but he made sure that he wasn't seen or recognised. He sat down by a fire in the courtyard to warm his hands.

What do you think he was thinking?

The High Priest brought forward many witnesses against Jesus. They tried to make out a case against him but their stories did not agree.

Why do you think this was?

When Jesus had spoken the High Priest tore his robes.

Why do you think this was?

Peter denies Jesus

AIMS

The aims of this section are to introduce:

1 The betrayal of Jesus by Peter

2 The theme of betrayal

3 Friendship and the demands it places upon us.

KEY WORDS

Disciple

Galilee

Gospel

High Priest

Peter

Matthew 26.69-75; Mark 14.66-72; Luke 22.56-62; John 18.15-18; 25-27

1 Whilst Jesus was being beaten and mocked, Peter remained in the courtyard of the High Priest's palace. The fact that he was there at all shows his concern for Jesus (no other disciple is mentioned) but this love could not bear the pressure placed on it by events. And it was Peter's Galilean accent that seemed to give him away as a follower of Jesus (Jesus also came from Galilee).

2 On two occasions Peter's friendship with Jesus was highlighted by a servant woman who had seen the two of them together. A third time the accusation came from the crowd and, on this occasion, Peter denied knowing Jesus at all. This third denial was followed by the second crowing of the rooster and a look from Jesus himself. This reminded him of what Jesus had predicted (Mark 14.27-31).

3 In recording this incident, the Gospel writers were warning their readers (in Mark's case those in Rome) that they would undergo persecution. The persecution instigated by Nero in AD 64 (in which both Peter and Paul died) was the first serious attempt by the Roman authorities to wipe out the Church. Mark wanted to warn Christians that if it was possible for the leader of the disciples to deny Jesus then it was possible for anyone, given sufficient provocation. They must be constantly on their guard. Yet the end of the story, in which Peter was forgiven, was a promise that if anyone failed then the door to forgiveness was always open (see Mark 16.7).

THE STORY

When Jesus was arrested he was taken to the palace of the High Priest. Peter followed him there and began to warm his hands in the courtyard of the palace. A servant woman recognised Peter as a follower of Jesus and said so, loudly. Peter denied it. Just then a rooster crowed. After a little while the woman began to tell people in the crowd that Peter was a follower of Jesus. Again, Peter denied it. People in the crowd began to accuse Peter. "Surely you are a follower of Jesus. Your accent tells us that you come from Galilee, just like Jesus does". This was too much for Peter, who was very afraid of the crowd. He began to swear that he had never even met Jesus.

Just then the rooster crowed for a second time. Peter remembered what Jesus had told him a few days earlier. Before the rooster crows twice, Jesus had said, you will deny me three times. At the time Peter had boasted that he would die for Jesus rather than deny him. Now Peter knew how empty that boast had been. He left the courtyard and cried with shame.

DISCUSSION POINTS

1 *The Bible story of Peter's denial of Jesus.*

2 *The meaning of the word 'betrayal'.* You may need to clarify this for the children. Talk about the context in which Jesus was betrayed by Peter.

3 *The meaning of friendship.* What does friendship mean? Why do friends hurt each other? Why did Peter hurt Jesus? What did forgiveness mean to Peter? How do we forgive?

 NAME..

Jesus betrayed by his friends

Mark 14.53-62 and Mark 14.66-72.

1. Why do you think that Judas betrayed Jesus ?

2. Why do you think that Peter betrayed Jesus?

3. Have you ever let a friend down badly?

If so, what happened?

In both of the passages, Jesus is betrayed by a close friend.

4. Has a friend let you down?

If so, what happened?

5. Did you forgive them?

Jesus is brought before Pilate

AIMS

The aims of this section are to introduce:

1 Pilate and his role in the Roman Empire

2 The attitude of Jesus towards the accusations that were made against him

3 The attempt by Pilate to release Barabbas instead of Jesus.

KEY WORDS

Barabbas
Blasphemy
Gospels
Jerusalem
Luke
Passover
Pilate
Sanhedrin

Matthew 27.1-28; Mark 15.1-15; Luke 23.1-25; John 18.28-40; 29.1-16

1 The Sanhedrin decided not to accuse Jesus of blasphemy since the Romans did not consider that to be a crime. They settled instead for a charge of high treason. This was a charge that no Roman Governor could possibly overlook. Jesus, who had disappointed the crowds by failing to lead a political uprising against the Romans, was now accused of that very crime.

2 The official residence of the Roman Governors of Judea was at Caesarea on the Mediterranean coast. Whenever the Roman Governors came to Jerusalem they lived in the Palace of Herod and this was where Jesus was taken. The Roman Governor would be available to deal with the matter early in the morning. (This explains why the Sanhedrin held their meeting late at night and early in the morning.)

3 According to Luke, the Sanhedrin brought three charges against Jesus:
- he was subverting the nation
- he opposed the payment of taxes to Caesar.
- he claimed to be the Christ (the King).

It was the third of these charges that interested Pilate. He asked Jesus directly, "Are you the King of the Jews?". Jesus simply replied, "So you say". He said nothing else. Pilate could not find him guilty of any of the crimes.

4 The custom of releasing a prisoner at Passover time is unknown (although it is not impossible) outside the Gospels. Pilate attempted to use the custom to release Jesus but was totally unsuccessful. The crowd demanded the release of Barabbas (a murderer and a thief). Pilate handed Jesus over to be flogged.

THE STORY

Jesus was taken from the Sanhedrin to the house of the Roman Governor. The Roman Governor's name was Pontius Pilate and he was known to be a very cruel man. Jesus came before him very early in the morning. The accusers of Jesus told Pilate that they had heard Jesus telling the people all kinds of things. Jesus, they said, told the people that they were not to pay taxes to the Roman Emperor in Rome. They also said he claimed to be the King of the Jews. This frightened Pilate but Jesus said almost nothing. Pilate wanted to set Jesus free but he was told that the people were beginning to riot.

Suddenly Pilate had a bright idea. At this time of the year the governor always set a prisoner free. Perhaps the people would take Jesus. He made the suggestion to them. But the people, wanted him to release a murderer called Barabbas. Pilate could not change their minds. Barabbas was released. Pilate handed Jesus over to be put to death.

DISCUSSION POINTS

1 *The Bible story of Jesus being brought before Pilate.*

2 *The way that the law works in this country.* Does the law always get it right and treat people fairly? Talk about miscarriages of justice. Why do we have 'trial by jury'?

3 *The trial of Jesus.* Was that a 'miscarriage of justice'? Why did Pilate condemn Jesus to death?

See Factsheet 3, page 12.

NAME...

Jesus and Pilate

Read Mark 15.1-15.

Draw Pilate.
Write down four things that you know about him.

1. ______________________________

____

____

2. ______________________________

____

____

3. ______________________________

____

____

4. ______________________________

____

____

Draw Jesus.
Write down four things that you know about him.

1. ______________________________

____

____

2. ______________________________

____

____

3. ______________________________

____

____

4. ______________________________

____

____

The death of Jesus

AIMS

The aims of this section are to introduce:

1 The Gospel story of the death of Jesus

2 The reasons why this story is at the heart of the Christian faith

3 The way in which the events surrounding the death of Jesus affected those people who were most closely involved.

KEY WORDS

Golgotha	Pilate
Gospels	Simon of Cyrene
Jerusalem	Stations of the Cross
Luke	Vigil
Messiah	

Matthew 27.32-44; Mark 15.21-32; Luke 23.26-43; John 19.17-27

1 In their accounts of the crucifixion of Jesus, the four Gospels tell essentially the same story although they differ in some of the details and in the words of Jesus that they record. None of the accounts concentrate on the physical agonies of Jesus and the suggestion is that this should not be our focus either. What matters far more is the spiritual anguish into which Jesus was entering. At the same time, it is important to answer children's questions about the physical pain involved as they arise.

2 Just like others condemned to death by the Romans, Jesus was required to carry his heavy cross to the place of execution. He was already weakened by the beating that he had received. This is why Simon of Cyrene, from a port in North Africa, was pressed into service to help him carry the cross.

3 Jesus was executed alongside two criminals, emphasising the humiliation that crucifixion involved and stressing the companionship which Jesus had, throughout his life, with outsiders. Luke records that one of the criminals 'hurled insults' at Jesus whilst the other asked Jesus to remember him when he entered paradise. Luke also records Jesus's prayer for those who carried out the sentence, "Forgive them, Father! They don't know what they are doing." (23.34). Luke also states that the religious leaders said of Jesus, "He saved others; let him save himself if he is the Messiah whom God has chosen." (Luke 23.35).

THE STORY

After Jesus had been condemned he was led out of Pilate's palace with two other criminals towards a place called Golgotha, which means 'The place of the skull'. By this time Jesus was very weak but he was expected to carry his cross. He couldn't manage so the soldiers pulled someone out of the crowd, Simon of Cyrene, to help him carry the cross.

On the cross the men's clothes were taken and shared out amongst the soldiers. Jesus prayed that those who were hurting them might be forgiven by God. Some of those standing around the cross called out very unkind things to Jesus. One of the criminals dying with him said, "If you are who you say you are, then save yourself and save us too." But the second criminal asked Jesus to remember him when he reached heaven. Then something very unusual happened. The sun was blotted out and the whole earth became totally dark for hours. Jesus cried out in a loud voice to God, trusting himself to God's safe keeping. Then he died. One of the soldiers standing by the cross said that Jesus was a good man. Some of the followers of Jesus were there and saw him die.

DISCUSSION POINTS

1 *The Bible story of the crucifixion of Jesus.*

2 *Children's experiences of acute disappointment.* Talk about the emotions which the disciples, and others, must have experienced as they saw Jesus dying. (Use Copymaster 29.)

3 *How different Christian Churches re-enact the last few hours of the life of Jesus* (marches with crosses; pilgrimages up the Via Dolorosa, the way of sorrows, in Jerusalem; vigil services; visiting the different Stations of the Cross, etc.)

 NAME...

What were they feeling?

Each of the people below were involved in some way in the death of Jesus.

What do you think they were feeling when they realised that Jesus was dead?

The disciples

Judas Iscariot

Mary, Jesus's mother

Simon of Cyrene

The soldier

Peter

Pontius Pilate

The religious leaders

The resurrection of Jesus

AIMS

The aims of this section are to introduce:

1 The story of Jesus rising from the dead

2 The range of emotions that the disciples felt between Good Friday and Easter Sunday

3 The strong Christian tradition that women were the first people to meet and speak with the risen Christ.

KEY WORDS

Easter	Mary Magdalene
Eucharist	Maundy Thursday
Galilee	Peter
Good Friday	Sabbath Day
Joseph of Arithmathea	

Matthew 28.1-10; Mark 16.1-8; Luke 24.1-9; John 20.1-18

1 Jesus had to be buried before the Jewish Sabbath day started at sunset on the Friday. This left no time for the body to be anointed with oil as was the usual custom. Mary and her two companions went to the tomb to carry out this task first thing on the Sunday morning.

2 In pre-Christian times the word Easter was associated with the Goddess of Spring and the rebirth of the natural world after the barren winter. In the Christian Church, Easter celebrates the death and resurrection of Jesus Christ. Church services on Easter Day are joyful and many include a celebration of the Eucharist. This special meal will not have been celebrated in church since Maundy Thursday. During the Eucharist on Easter Day the priest or vicar proclaims to the people 'Christ is risen', to which the congregation responds, 'He is risen indeed'. In other Churches a special service is held at sunrise to welcome the risen Christ.

THE STORY

The Sabbath day had started almost as soon as Jesus had died on Good Friday. No work was done on the Sabbath day and so nobody had visited the tomb of Joseph of Arithmathea where the body of Jesus had been laid. As soon as the Sabbath day was over, however, three women visited the tomb. One of them was called Mary Magdalene. In those days a tomb was carved out of a rock and had a large stone rolled across its entrance. It usually took several men to roll the stone away to one side.

When the women arrived at the tomb, however, they could not believe what they saw. The stone had already been rolled away and an angel, dressed in white, was sitting inside. There was no sign of the body of Jesus. The angel spoke to the women. He said that Jesus was no longer dead. God had brought him back to life. The angel told the women to go and tell Peter and the other disciples that Jesus would meet them in Galilee. Mary Magdalene then saw Jesus walking about in the garden but she did not recognise him. She thought he was the gardener. When Mary heard him speak her name she knew who it was. Jesus had come back to life and she was the first person to see him.

DISCUSSION POINTS

1 *The Bible story of the resurrection of Jesus.* Describe how Jesus appeared to Mary Magdalene and the other women.

2 *A walk.* Look for the signs of Spring, listen to the sounds, sniff the smells. Draw out ideas from bird-song, birds building nests, grass growing, signs of life in ponds, etc. Draw a parallel between the new life of Spring and the resurrection of Jesus.

3 *A tableau.* Depict the arrival of Peter and John at the tomb or the encounter of Mary with Jesus.

 NAME...

Jesus rises from the dead

Read Matthew 28.1-10; Mark 16.1-8; Luke 24.1-9; John 20.1-18.
Each of the four Gospels tell us about the resurrection of Jesus from the dead.

Look at each Gospel account and answer the questions below.
Leave a blank if there is nothing in a particular Gospel about an event.
Write on a separate page if you need to.

	Matthew	*Mark*	*Luke*	*John*
1. Who went to the tomb of Jesus?				
2. When did they visit the tomb?				
3. What made them go?				
4. What did they see at the tomb?				
5. What did they hear at the tomb?				
6. What did they do afterwards?				

The walk to Emmaus

AIMS

The aims of this section are to introduce:

1 The Bible story of the walk that Jesus took with two followers to the village of Emmaus

2 The way in which their eyes were opened to recognise Jesus in the breaking of bread.

KEY WORDS

Disciple	Moses
Jerusalem	Palm Sunday
Luke	Passover
Messiah	Prophet

Mark 16.12,13; Luke 24.13-35

1 The identities of the two followers of Jesus who accompanied him on the walk to Emmaus are not revealed in Luke's account. Clearly they were not disciples but were amongst those followers who had come to Jerusalem for the Passover festival. They were probably in the group that had welcomed Jesus into the city on Palm Sunday and who were now making their way home, very dispirited.

2 As the two followers travelled home they were discussing Jesus and their belief that he had been the Messiah who would usher in God's Kingdom. When Jesus joined them they continued walking without recognising him (the reason for this is not given). Asked why they were sad the couple expressed their belief that Jesus had been a prophet sent by God. They also mentioned the rumour that some women had gone to the tomb early in the morning and found it empty. Jesus rebuked them for their lack of faith when it was plainly written in the Jewish Scriptures, "beginning with the books of Moses and the writings of all the prophets . . ." (Luke 24.27) that the Messiah must suffer and die before entering into his glory.

3 The invitation to Jesus to stay the night with them followed the custom of Eastern hospitality. Surprisingly, Jesus played the part of host and broke the bread before eating. This reminded the two followers of the feeding of the 5,000 and they realised who their guest was. The narrative ended abruptly with Jesus disappearing.

THE STORY

On the day that Jesus returned from the dead, two of his followers were going home. They lived in Emmaus, a village about 11 kilometres from Jerusalem. They had seen Jesus die and were very sad. Jesus joined them on the walk but they did not realise who he was. By the time the three of them came to Emmaus, it was getting dark and the two followers asked Jesus to stay the night with them.

Jesus went into their house. A meal was prepared and set on the table in front of Jesus. He took a loaf of bread from the table and broke it in pieces to give to them. They had seen Jesus do exactly the same thing when he had fed a large number of people from just five loaves and two fish. They looked again at the person in front of them. Finally they realised who their guest was. How could they have been so blind? It could only be Jesus. They recognised him but, as they did so, he disappeared. They ran all the way back to Jerusalem to tell the disciples what had happened. Jesus wasn't dead any more. He was alive.

DISCUSSION POINTS

1 *The Bible story of the resurrection of Jesus.*

2 *Occasions on which the children have been very sad.* What made you so unhappy? Why? What made these two followers of Jesus so sad? What changed their lives?

3 *An imaginary walk.* Think about where you are going. Imagine that you are suddenly aware that someone is walking alongside you. It is Jesus but you do not realise it. You tell him what has upset you. He listens to what you are saying. What does he say to you?

See Factsheet 18, page 27.

 NAME...

The two friends

Read Luke 24.13-35.

Answer these questions. Luke 24.13-35 will help you.

1. Where was Emmaus?

2. What were the two friends talking about as they walked to Emmaus?

3. How were the two friends feeling?

4. What did the stranger tell them?

5. Who was the stranger?

6. How did they realise who was with them?

Jesus appears to his disciples

AIMS

The aims of this section are to introduce:

1 Some of the people to whom Jesus is said to have appeared

2 The appearance of Jesus to his terrified disciples.

Matthew 28.16-20; Mark 16.14-18; Luke 24.36-49; John 20.19-23

1 According to the Gospels, and Paul's first letter to the Corinthians, Jesus appeared many times after he rose from the dead. He appeared to Mary Magdalene at the tomb, to Peter in Jerusalem, to the ten disciples in the Upper Room, to disciples fishing on the Sea of Galilee, and to all the disciples on a mountain.

2 The Gospel of Luke opens with a terrified Zechariah (1.12) and ends with the terrified disciples (24.37). The disciples are terrified because they think that they are seeing a ghost but Jesus draws attention to the fact that he is really flesh and bones. He then sets out to prove that he has really risen from the dead by asking if they have anything to eat. Jesus explains to them that everything that he said to them before his death has come true.

KEY WORDS

Disciple	New Testament
Gospels	Paul
Holy Spirit	Peter
Jerusalem	Sea of Galilee
Luke	Zechariah
Mary Magdalene	

3 This particular episode goes further, however. Not only does Jesus appear to show that he has risen from the dead but he also gives his disciples a commission, "in his name the message about repentance and forgiveness of sins must be preached to all nations, beginning in Jerusalem" (Luke 24.47). At that time, however, the disciples were in no fit state to carry this out. They were to wait in Jerusalem until God's Holy Spirit visited them. This was to happen on the Day of Pentecost (Acts 2).

THE STORY

Do you remember what the two followers of Jesus did when they met him in Emmaus? As soon as Jesus disappeared they went back to Jerusalem quickly to tell the disciples that they had seen Jesus. As they were doing so, Jesus suddenly appeared to all of the disciples. They were absolutely terrified. They thought that they were seeing a ghost. But Jesus soon put their minds at rest. "Look at my hands and feet, he said, and you will see that I am not a ghost. Feel me and you will discover that I am flesh and bones. You cannot touch a ghost."

The disciples were overcome with happiness. They didn't know what to do with themselves. To show them that he wasn't a ghost he ate a piece of fish. Then he began to explain to them something very important. "Whatever you read in your Scriptures," he said, "has now come true. I suffered and died but now I have come back to life. My work is almost finished but your work is just beginning. You must carry the message that I have given to you and pass it on to others. You must start doing this in the city of Jerusalem. But don't rush out straight away. The work can only begin when you have received God's Holy Spirit."

That happened, as the New Testament tells us, on the Day of Pentecost.

DISCUSSION POINTS

1 *The Bible story of Jesus appearing to the disciples.*

2 *Feelings of doubt.* Imagine that you are one of the disciples. You have heard several reports that Jesus is alive. You still can't help having some doubts about whether he is. What would remove those doubts once and for all?

3 *Doubting Thomas.* Discuss the use of this term today and read children the story.

 NAME..

Questions about Jesus

Look at each description below and write the right words next to it. Number four has been done for you, as an example. You will find all the answers in Luke chapters 22, 23 and 24.

1. The last meal that Jesus ate with his friends. ______________

2. Jesus blessed and broke this at the Last Supper. ______________

3. He died on a cross. ______________

4. Jesus walked there with his friends. ✎ *Emmaus*

5. He denied Jesus. ______________

6. Jesus died on this. ______________

7. A special messenger from God. ______________

8. The women told them that Jesus had risen. ______________

9. He watched the death of Jesus from a distance. ______________

10. The day that Jesus died. ______________

11. The body of Jesus was placed in this. ______________

12. The day that Jesus rose from the dead. ______________

Unit Three: The miracles of Jesus

The wedding at Cana

AIMS

The aims of this section are to introduce:

1 The miracle which, according to John, was the first that Jesus performed

2 The social disaster of the hosts running out of wine

3 The relationship between Jesus and his mother (his independence and her obedience)

4 The effect that witnessing the miracle had on the disciples.

KEY WORDS

Disciple	John
Galilee	Miracle
Gospel	Nazareth

John 2.1-12

1 John is the only Gospel writer to record this incident. Cana was a village in the hills of Galilee, about nine miles north of Nazareth. In a small village like Cana a marriage would be a very important community occasion. Wine would be a central part of the celebration and the failure to provide it would be a social disgrace. For this occasion the mother of Jesus, Mary, and the disciples were also present.

2 Mary informs her son that the wine has run out. The reply Jesus gives her appears brusque but she tells the servants to do exactly as he says. By this action she implies that he is no longer under her authority but receiving his authority directly from God. The six stone jars filled with water held about twenty gallons each. Most of the water would normally be provided for the guests to wash their hands before eating. No miracle is described. The water is drawn out of the jars and by the time that it is tasted by the man in charge of the feast it has become wine. Not only wine but the best wine of the feast. (Generally the best wine was served first and that of a poorer quality served later when the taste of the guests had been dulled.)

3 To John, the miracles of Jesus were all signs. Just as the water (used for Jewish purification) was turned into wine so Jesus, he believed, had come to replace the old order with the new. His miracles were signs that God was with him.

THE STORY

Jesus had just called his first disciples. Amongst those who had started to follow him were Peter, Andrew, Philip and Nathaniel. He went with them, and his mother, to a wedding reception in a small village called Cana. Whilst they were there something terrible happened. The reception ran out of wine. This was particularly serious because Eastern wedding receptions went on for many days. Mary told Jesus what had happened before telling the servants at the reception to do whatever Jesus, her son, told them.

In those days everyone was expected to wash their hands before each course of a feast. The water for this was stored in very large stone jars. Jesus told the servants to fill six of these jars with water up to the brim. They did so. They were then told to take some water out and present it to the person in charge of the feast. When he tasted it he found that the water had been turned into wine. Having taken a sip he declared it to be a better wine than the one they had already drunk. Everyone was very happy. This was the first miracle of Jesus.

DISCUSSION POINTS

1 *The Bible story of the first miracle.*

2 *A modern wedding reception.* How would this be different from the one that Jesus attended? What could happen that would bring social disgrace to a reception today? How would guests feel if the wine ran out?

 NAME..

The wedding feast

Read John 2.1-12.

Have you ever been to a wedding reception? How do Christians celebrate a wedding?

Imagine you are at the wedding reception in Cana. What is happening?

UNIT THREE

Healing a paralysed man and a leper

AIMS

The aims of this section are to introduce:

1 The miracle of Jesus healing a leper (described as a man with 'a dreaded skin disease')

2 The miracle of Jesus healing the paralysed man let down through the roof by four of his friends

3 The link between the forgiveness of sins and the healing of the body.

KEY WORDS

Blasphemy	Leprosy
Capernaum	Miracle
Galilee	Teachers of the Law

Mark 1.40-45; Mark 2.1-12

1 *Mark 1.40-45.* The word 'leprosy' was used in Biblical times to denote a wide range of skin diseases, many of which were not contagious. The Jewish law laid down a clear requirement for people with such diseases (Leviticus 13.45,46). The man in this story, instead of keeping his distance from Jesus as the law demanded, fell on his knees in front of him. He knew that Jesus could heal him but he was not sure that he would. Jesus touched the man and the disease left him 'at once' (a favourite word of Mark's). Jesus 'sternly' charged the man to say nothing but the man began to spread the news everywhere. As a result Jesus could no longer enter any of the towns publicly.

2 *Mark 2.1-12.* This miracle is intended to show the close connection between the healing of the body and the forgiveness of sins (the physical and the spiritual). Jesus went to Capernaum and entered a house there. The news soon spread that he was in the town and the house filled with people. Four friends brought a paralysed man to Jesus but, when they could not enter the house, let him down through the roof. In flat-topped Eastern houses this was perfectly possible. Jesus saw the faith of the four friends but, instead of healing the man, he forgave his sins. The 'teachers of the law' who were there believed that only God could forgive sins. They did not believe that Jesus was divine and so what he was claiming to do was blasphemy to them. Blasphemy was to be the religious sin on which the Sanhedrin condemned Jesus (page 76).

THE STORY

A man suffering from a terrible skin disease came and fell at the feet of Jesus, hoping to be cured. Jesus was full of pity for the man. The man's life had been very unhappy because of his illness. People would not go near him and he was alone. Jesus touched him and the disease went away. Jesus told the man not to tell anyone what had happened but the man could not keep the news to himself. The news spread like wildfire. Soon many people wanted to meet Jesus.

Shortly afterwards, Jesus went to a town called Capernaum. People crowded into the house where he was. A paralysed man on a stretcher hoped to see Jesus but there were too many people. So four of his friends carried him up on to the flat roof and let him down at the feet of Jesus. Jesus told the man that his sins were forgiven. This upset some people as only God could forgive sins. Jesus then told the man that his disease had been healed as well and he walked out of the house. As you can imagine, everyone was amazed.

DISCUSSION POINTS

1 *The Bible stories of the two miracles.*

2 *The friends of the paralysed man.* Why did the man need help? Could he have been healed without help? What was special about his friends? How did they show their love? Encourage children to reflect on the loneliness which the first man must have had to endure.

3 *Forgiveness.* What is forgiveness? How do we forgive? Are forgiving and forgetting the same? Is it easy to forgive? How do people hurt God? What does this story teach us about God's forgiveness?

 NAME..

Jesus at work

Mark 1.40-45 and 2.1-12.

1. What was wrong with this man?

2. What did the man do when he met Jesus?

3. How did Jesus heal him?

4. What did the man do after Jesus healed him?

1. Why did this man's friends want to reach Jesus?

2. How did he reach Jesus?

3. What did Jesus say to him and what did others say?

4. How did Jesus heal him?

The centurion's servant

AIMS

The aims of this section are to introduce:

1 The Roman occupation of Palestine

2 The humility and faith of the Roman centurion

3 The admiration of Jesus for the centurion

4 The healing of the centurion's servant without Jesus visiting his home.

KEY WORDS

Capernaum	Matthew
Gospels	Palestine
Judaism	

Matthew 8.5-13; Luke 7.1-10

1 The Romans had occupied Palestine since 63 BC. Centurions formed the backbone of the occupying forces. They maintained discipline and also carried out the orders passed down from Rome. Therefore the centurion in the story feels he is unworthy of Jesus and declines his offer to come to his house. The comment of the officer is also taken by Jesus to show a degree of faith which, according to Jesus, was greater than anything he found within his own community.

2 The words which Jesus apparently directed against those who had the benefit of being brought up in the Jewish faith are unlikely to have actually come from Jesus. The anti-Jewish sentiments (which are surprisingly common in the Gospels) almost certainly come from a much later stage when the Christian Church was trying to make it clear to the Romans that it had severed its links with Judaism.

3 Because of the centurion's faith, Jesus went ahead and healed his servant. The centurion was then told to return home. Matthew informs us that the servant was healed from 'that very moment'.

THE STORY

Jesus entered the town of Capernaum. As he did so he was met by a Roman centurion. (A centurion was in charge of 100 soldiers.) The centurion approached Jesus to tell him that his servant was in bed, sick, unable to move and suffering terribly. Jesus said that he would come to the centurion's house but this alarmed the soldier. He told Jesus that he was not worthy for him to even set foot inside his house. Instead, Jesus could just give the word and his servant would be healed. As he explained to Jesus, he was used to giving orders and expecting them to be obeyed.

Jesus was amazed by what the man told him. He turned to the people following him and told them that he had never come across such faith before. He turned to the centurion. "Go home," he said to him, "what you believe will happen to you". The man left him. When he reached his home he found that his servant was perfectly well. He had been cured at the exact moment that Jesus had spoken to him.

DISCUSSION POINTS

1 *The Bible story of the centurion's servant.*

2 *A Roman soldier's life.* Why were orders always carried out at once? Would a soldier disobey orders? How did this centurion approach Jesus? Why did he not want Jesus to set foot inside his house?

3 *Faith.* What is faith? How do we all exercise faith each day? What was special about the centurion's faith? How did it show itself? Why was Jesus so surprised by what the man said?

COPYMASTER 33 NAME...

The Roman centurion

Read Matthew 8.5-13.

Fill in the missing words.

Jesus entered the town of ____________ . He was met by a Roman ____________ who was very worried about his ____________ . Jesus said that he would go to the centurion's ____________ to heal the man. The centurion said that he was not worthy for this to happen. Jesus only needed to say the ____________ and his ____________ would be ____________ .

Capernaum	servant	centurion	healed	house	servant	words

Draw a picture to go with each of the sentences below.

1. Jesus entered Capernaum with a crowd following him.

2. He was approached by a Roman centurion.

3. The centurion asked Jesus to heal his servant.

4. The centurion found that his servant had been healed.

Making Bartimaeus see

AIMS

The aims of this section are to introduce:

1 How the blind man, Bartimaeus, took the initiative in seeking help from Jesus

2 The response of the people around

3 The response of Jesus to human need.

KEY WORDS

Disciple	Matthew
Jericho	Messiah
Jerusalem	Nazareth
Luke	Son of David
Mark	

Matthew 20.29-34; Mark 10.46-52; Luke 18.35-43

1 This incident took place as Jesus was drawing near to the town of Jericho, about 25 km from Jerusalem. This is the last recorded miracle in the ministry of Jesus. Luke recorded that the miracle occurred as Jesus entered Jericho from the north, Matthew and Mark believed it happened as he left the city and was heading south.

2 In this story, physical sight is also a metaphor for spiritual sight, or understanding. Bartimaeus was physically blind but he recognised Jesus to be the promised Messiah ('the Son of David'). When the people, who were spiritually blind but physically sighted, tried to silence him, he made his presence more strongly felt. As Jesus had said at the beginning of his ministry (Luke 4.18) he would make the blind see. The blind man knew that something special was about to take place – the triumphal entry of Jesus into Jerusalem was only a day or two away (Luke 19.29-40).

3 The description of Bartimaeus insisting on calling out to Jesus underlines the man's faith. When Jesus heals Bartimaeus he makes it clear that it is the faith of Bartimaeus that has brought about the healing. Only Luke speaks of the praise that both the blind man and the people gave to God after the miracle.

THE STORY

One day, towards the end of his life, Jesus was leaving the city of Jericho with his disciples. A large crowd of people were following behind. A blind man, Bartimaeus, was sitting by the roadside begging. He did this every day because he couldn't work and had no money to buy food. When he heard the crowd getting more and more excited around him he asked someone what was going on. He was told that Jesus, from Nazareth, was passing by. This made Bartimaeus excited because he had heard all about Jesus and the wonderful things that he did.

Bartimaeus began to call out. He called Jesus 'the Son of David'. The people around him told him to be quiet but Bartimaeus made even more noise. Jesus heard his voice and stopped. He told one of his disciples to bring the blind man to him. Jesus asked Bartimaeus what he would like him to do. Bartimaeus told Jesus that he would like to be able to see again. Jesus told him that he would be healed because of his great faith. At once, Bartimaeus could see. He joined the crowd that was following Jesus.

DISCUSSION POINTS

1 *The Bible story of making Bartimaeus see.* This story can be dramatised effectively with the children playing the main parts and also forming the crowd. Take time to explore the feelings of the different characters in the drama.

2 *What it means to be blind.* Some of them can try to make their way from one side of the classroom to the other wearing a blindfold.

3 *Disability.* Discuss how a blind person might manage in your area (obstacles, difficulties, dangers, etc.). You may be able to arrange a visit from a blind person with a guide-dog.

Bartimaeus

Read Mark 10.46-52.
Link the words below to make four sentences.
Then copy the sentences out, in the right order, to tell the story of Jesus and Bartimaeus. The first one has been done for you.

1. Bartimaeus	*by a large group of people.*
Jesus was followed	*Bartimaeus could see again.*
Jesus	*was a blind man who begged by the roadside.*
After Jesus healed him	*was leaving Jericho.*

✎ *Bartimaeus was a blind man who begged by the roadside.*

2. Imagine that you were there. Describe Jesus healing Bartimaeus.

3. Describe how regaining his sight could change Bartimaeus's life.

UNIT THREE

The man with the paralysed hand

AIMS

The aims of this section are to introduce:

1 The Sabbath day

2 The questions that Jesus directed towards his opponents

3 The anger and pity of Jesus for his opponents

4 The healing of the man with the paralysed hand.

KEY WORDS

Herod

Herodians

Mark

Pharisees

Sabbath Day

Synagogue

Synoptic Gospels

Matthew 12.9-14; Mark 3.1-6; Luke 6.6-11

1 This story, recorded by all three Synoptic Gospels, is a conflict which Jesus has with the religious authorities over observing the Sabbath day. Mark has already recorded Jesus as saying, "The Sabbath was made for the good of human beings; they were not made for the Sabbath" (2.27). He applies this principle to the case of a man with a paralysed hand who came to him for healing on the Sabbath day. The Jewish law allowed healing on the Sabbath – but only if a person's life was in danger. That was clearly not the case here. Mark tells us that 'some people' watched Jesus very closely to see whether he broke this law.

2 Instead of acting carefully Jesus brought the man forward, asking his opponents whether life should be saved or destroyed, helped or harmed on the Sabbath day. The questions were not directly related to the situation of the man. His opponents said nothing. Their attitude made Jesus angry, an emotion rarely attributed to him in the Gospels. Jesus then told the man to stretch out his hand and he was healed.

3 The healing of the man led to further enmity against Jesus. The Pharisees were joined by the Herodians (probably influential people who supported the family of Herod) and together they began to plot the arrest and death of Jesus. This conspiracy is mentioned here for the first time. It reappears three more times (in Mark 11.18; 12.12 and 14.1).

THE STORY

One day, Jesus visited a synagogue. (This is the building in which Jewish people meet to worship God.) He went there on the Sabbath day. This is the most special day of the week for all Jewish people. Many Jewish people do not do any kind of work on the Sabbath day. Jesus was Jewish.

A man with a paralysed hand approached Jesus. The hand was causing the man pain but his life was not in any kind of danger. Jewish laws at that particular time many, many years ago, prevented a person healing someone on the Sabbath day unless their life was in danger. The opponents of Jesus watched Jesus, to see what he would do. Jesus turned to them and asked them what was the best thing to do on the Sabbath day, God's holy day. Was it to help or to harm someone? Was it to save someone's life or to destroy it? His opponents did not say anything.

Jesus turned to the man. "Stretch out your hand," he said to him. The man did as he was told and his hand was healed. The opponents of Jesus began to talk with each other. They wanted to discuss how they could get Jesus arrested.

DISCUSSION POINTS

1 *The Bible story of Jesus and healing on the Sabbath.*

2 *Special days.* Link special days celebrated by the children with the Sabbath as it is celebrated by Jewish people today. Explain why it is a 'day of rest'. What is the value of this? Link the Sabbath with Sunday.

See Factsheets 5, 7 and 8 on pages 14, 16 and 17.

COPYMASTER 35 NAME..

A healing on the Sabbath

Read Mark 3.1-6.

1. Where was Jesus?

2. Who did Jesus meet?

3. What did the onlookers wait to see?

4. Why were the people watching him carefully?

5. What was the special day?

6. What did Jesus say to the man with the paralysed hand?

7. Jesus said:
"What does our Law allow us to do on the Sabbath? To help or to harm? To save someone's life or to destroy it?"
Explain this in your own words.

8. Why was Jesus angry?

9. What did Jesus do to the man with the paralysed hand?

The sick man by the pool

AIMS

The aims of this section are to introduce:

1 The helplessness of the sick and needy in the time of Jesus

2 The selection by Jesus of just one man among many to heal (the man had been ill for 38 years)

3 The man's instantaneous cure

4 The controversy over healing on the Sabbath.

KEY WORDS

Angel

Jerusalem

Sabbath Day

John 5.1-14

1 The pool referred to in the story is probably the one located by archaeologists in the north-west corner of the old city of Jerusalem. The pool was surrounded by a colonnade on all four sides and down the centre of the pool. People gathered at the water's edge hoping to be cured of their illnesses when the waters were stirred up. Local superstition suggested that the first person into the water after this happened was cured.

2 Jesus seemed to have selected to heal the person who was the most needy. A paralysed man who did not have anyone to help him into the water had lain there for 38 years. Being confined to his bed for so long would have prevented the man from helping himself. In the light of this, Jesus's question, "Do you want to get well?", would seem to have been unnecessary. But Jesus may have been trying to see whether the man had a will to be cured, a kind of faith.

3 Jesus asked the man to do the impossible: to stand on his feet, pick up his bed-roll and walk. The man did so. As with so many miracles, however, this became a 'conflict story' bringing Jesus into conflict with the Jewish authorities of the time. As so often this turned out to be a conflict over Sabbath observance. On this occasion, the man was breaking the strict Sabbath laws by carrying his bed on the Sabbath.

THE STORY

In the city of Jerusalem there was a pool. It had five porches and sick people of all kinds lay in them on stretchers. There were blind people, people who could not walk and others who could not even stand up. They were there because of a local story. This story said that, from time to time, an angel came down and stirred up the waters of the pool. The story went on to say that the first person into the water when this happened would be cured. A person could only be first in the pool if he or she had someone to help them.

One man who was paralysed and could not move, had lain at the side of the pool for 38 years. There was nobody to help him into the water quickly and so he had not been cured. When Jesus walked by he asked the man whether he wanted to be cured. Jesus then told him to get to his feet, roll up his bed under his arm and walk away. The man did as he was told. He was cured. But it happened to be the Sabbath, the day of the week on which no work was to be done. To the religious leaders work included carrying a bed. They were very annoyed with Jesus because of what he had done.

DISCUSSION POINTS

1 *The Bible story of the sick man by the pool.*

2 *What must it have been like to be paralysed for 38 years?* What would you miss most? How would you manage? How much would you depend on your friends and relations? Would you still hope to be cured after all that time?

3 *The Jewish law allowing a person to be cured on the Sabbath if their life was in danger.* Was the life of this man in danger? Could Jesus have waited to cure him? Why didn't he? Why didn't such laws seem to interest Jesus? What might the law have been there for? (e.g. to keep the day special, preserve family life, etc.)

See Factsheets 5 and 8 on pages 14 and 17.

 NAME..

The pool

Read John 5.1-18.

There was an old story about a pool in Jerusalem.
The pool was thought to have miraculous powers.
Write what the old story said about the pool.

____

____

____

____

____

Fill in the missing words below.

One day Jesus walked past the pool. The pool had ________ porches. People who were ill were laying in the porches. Some ____________ , some were ____________ and some were __________ . One man had laid there for ___________ years. Jesus asked him ____ .

The man replied:

____

____

____

____

____

Jesus told him to:

____

____

____

____

____

The man picked up his _____________ and began to walk. This miracle took place on the _____________ _______________.

The ten lepers

AIMS

The aims of this section are to introduce:

1 The miracle of Jesus healing ten people who had 'dreaded skin diseases'

2 The way in which such people were treated in the time of Jesus ('they stood at a distance')

3 The return of one man to give thanks to Jesus.

KEY WORDS

Disciple	High Priest
Galilee	Peter
Gospel	

Luke 17.11-19

1 This miracle is only found in Luke's Gospel. The main point of the story is to show this as an encounter between Jesus, a Jew, and a Samaritan. The Samaritans and the Jews had been sworn enemies for over three centuries and there was no contact between them. Lepers tended to live in groups avoiding all contact with those not afflicted but they did live close to populated areas in order to beg for alms.

2 A priest had to certify that a person was cured of leprosy. The order to these lepers to search out a priest was unlikely since the Samaritans were not bound by the same rules as the Jews. This incident is also strange since the story clearly commends one leper for returning to give thanks although Jesus has clearly told them all to go. The answer seems to be that the returning leper received more than just healing for his body, he found true salvation. The others simply had their leprosy cured. This miracle emphasises, as do many others, that it is the faith of the person which has brought about their cure. "Your faith has made you well" is the key-note of many Gospel miracles.

THE STORY

Jesus was travelling to the city of Jerusalem. It was in Jerusalem that he was going to die. To get to the city he went through the country between Galilee and Samaria. Just as he was about to enter a village along the way he was met by ten men. They were all suffering from a very bad skin disease called leprosy. Other people were afraid of catching this disease so these men had to live outside the village. They called out to Jesus from a distance. They wanted Jesus to take pity on them and help them.

Anyone who thought that he was cured of this disease had to show himself to a priest. The priest would then decide if he was cured or not. Jesus told them to go and show themselves to a priest. As they went to find a priest they were cured of their disease. One of them, a person from Samaria, returned to thank Jesus for what had happened. Jesus was very pleased about this, especially as the man had come from a foreign country. He wondered why the other nine hadn't come back as well. He told the man that his faith had made him well.

DISCUSSION POINTS

1 *The Bible story of the ten lepers.*

2 *The disease that the men were suffering from.* How would this have affected their lives? How would they have felt being deprived of much human contact? Why were they not allowed to come into normal contact with people? What were the people afraid of? How would the lives of the men be changed after Jesus healed them?

3 *The reaction of Jesus when one person turned to thank him.* Why was Jesus pleased? Why is saying 'thank-you' so important?

 NAME..

Ten people who needed help

When Jesus approached a village on his way to Jerusalem he was met by ten men who had terrible skin diseases. What did they call out to him?

Jesus told them that he would cure them. What did he tell them to do?

One of the lepers returned to thank Jesus for healing him. Why do you think he did that?

Nine of the lepers did not return to thank Jesus for healing them. Why do you think they forgot?

Two miracles

AIMS

The aims of this section are to introduce:

1 A miracle in which Jesus appears to bring a young girl back from the dead

2 A miracle in which Jesus heals a woman who had been seriously ill for 12 years.

KEY WORDS

James
John
Lake of Galilee
Peter
Synagogue
Synoptic Gospels

Matthew 9.18-26; Mark 5. 21-43; Luke 8. 40-56

1 The writers of the Synoptic Gospels bring together and interweave two miracles here. The connecting link between them is that of ritual uncleanness. According to Jewish law, any contact with a dead body or blood made a person ceremonially unclean.

2 Jesus was on the west side of the Lake of Galilee when he was interrupted by the urgent plea of an official of the local synagogue. The man fell at the feet of Jesus because his daughter was seriously ill and Jesus set out with the man to his house. They were interrupted by a woman in great need and during this interruption the news came through that the man's daughter had died. Ignoring this news Jesus went into the house, threw out the official mourners and entered the child's room with Peter, James and John, his closest friends. Indicating that the girl was not dead but only sleeping Jesus took her by the hand and told her to get up. If this was a case of Jesus bringing someone back from the dead then it corresponds with the stories of the widow's son at Nain (Luke 7.11-15) and Lazarus (John 11.1-44).

3 In between Jesus being approached by the Jewish official and reaching his house a woman who had been bleeding for twelve years touched his cloak, seeking healing. Jesus asked for the person who had touched him to identify herself and when she did he commended her faith, "My daughter," he said, "your faith has made you well. Go in peace and be healed of your trouble".

THE STORY

One day, Jesus was beside a lake with his disciples when a large crowd gathered around him. An important man, called Jairus, approached him and fell down at his feet. The young daughter of Jairus, just twelve years old, was seriously ill. The man wanted Jesus to come and heal her. Jesus set off, with his disciples, towards the man's house. As he was travelling, a woman in the crowd, who had been ill for a long time, touched the hem of his clothes, believing that this would make her better. Jesus stopped and turned around. "Who touched me?" he asked. His disciples told him that many people were touching him but Jesus waited. The woman came forward trembling but Jesus told her that her faith had made her better.

Just then friends of the important man arrived to tell him that his daughter had died. Jesus took no notice of them and went to the man's house where he found many people crying. "The girl is not dead," Jesus told them, "only asleep". When they laughed at him, Jesus put them outside. He went into the girl's room, took her hand and lifted her up. She was very much alive. She walked around the house and gave everyone something to eat.

DISCUSSION POINTS

1 *The Bible story of the two miracles.*

2 *How people feel when those close to them are very ill.* Why is it much worse when the person is a child? How must this man have felt?

3 *The action of the woman in the story.* Why might she have wanted to keep her action a secret? What motive might Jesus have had in making her action public knowledge?

See Factsheet 7, on page 16.

 NAME...

Help

Read Mark 5.21-43.

Jairus was an important man in the local synagogue. This was the building in which Jewish people worshipped God. His daughter was very ill and needed help from Jesus.

When Jairus came to Jesus he …

____

____

____

____

As Jesus was going to the house of Jairus a woman in the crowd who had been ill for a long time touched him. She felt that if she only touched him she would be cured.

When the woman who had been ill for a long time touched Jesus he said …

____

____

____

____

Jesus calms a storm

AIMS

The aims of this section are to introduce:

1 A miracle which shows the power of Jesus over nature

2 The extraordinary power which Christians believe that Jesus has over all aspects of life.

KEY WORDS

Disciples

Lake of Galilee

Synagogue

Matthew 8.23-27; Mark 4.35-41; Luke 8.22-28

The Sea of Galilee was notorious for its sudden winds, storms and squalls. The hills surrounding it funnelled the wind down to the lake where it whipped up the water. In this story there are three important points to notice:

1 Jesus slept while the storm raged. In direct contrast, the disciples were terrified. In other miracles Jesus has shown his authority over demons, illness and death. Now that authority is demonstrated over the unruly elements of nature. The contrast is drawn between the quiet calm of Jesus and the lack of faith shown by the disciples.

2 Jesus commands the sea to be 'muzzled'. He uses the same word of the demon possessed man in the synagogue. The implication is that Jesus is binding an evil power (the sea).

3 After the event the disciples are speechless at the power which Jesus has shown. They wonder aloud "Who is this man? Even the wind and the waves obey him".

THE STORY

Jesus and his disciples had been working very hard. They were very tired. They had healed many people who were ill, and they had taught large crowds of people about God. They decided to sail across to the other side of the Sea of Galilee. After they had climbed into the boat Jesus fell asleep. There were often storms on the Sea of Galilee and one sprung up while they were crossing. The disciples were very frightened because the waves were so high that they thought the boat would sink.

The disciples grabbed Jesus by the shoulders and shook him awake. Jesus stood up in the boat and spoke to the wind and waves. He told them to be quiet. The wind dropped at once and the waves quieted down. The disciples were amazed. They couldn't believe their eyes. Who was this man that even the wind and the waves obeyed his voice? But Jesus was not very pleased with them. He didn't think that they should have been so frightened. Why didn't they have faith that God would look after them?

DISCUSSION POINTS

1 *The Bible story of Jesus calming the storm.* Re-tell or act out the story.

2 *Personal situations in which the powers of nature seem to be frightening.* E.g. thunder and lightning, hailstorm, snow and ice, etc.

3 *The universal experience of fear.* What frightens us? What do we do when we are afraid?

 NAME...

The frightened disciples

Read Mark 4.35-41.

Complete the sentences using the words below.

1. Jesus and his disciples were sailing in a ____________. They were going from one side of the Sea of ____________________ to the other. Suddenly a ________________ blew up and the __________________ were very frightened. Jesus was __________ in the boat. His _____________ woke him up. He ___________ to the ____________ and all was quiet.

asleep	disciples	spoke	boat	wind	Galilee	storm	disciples

2. What do you think Jesus was trying to teach his disciples?

____

____

____

____

____

____

____

____

____

____

____

____

____

____

What do you think it would be like to be in the storm?

____

____

____

____

Jesus walks on water

AIMS

The aims of this section are to introduce:

1 A miracle to show the authority of Jesus over the power of nature

2 The concern that Jesus had for the welfare of his disciples

3 The lack of faith in Jesus shown by Peter

4 The recognition by the disciples that Jesus was God's Son.

KEY WORDS

Disciple

Messiah

Peter

Matthew 14.22-33; Mark 6.45-52; John 6.15-21

1 This incident is introduced by a reference to Jesus praying. According to John (6.15), after seeing him perfom a miracle, the people were attempting to make him a king by force and this may have been the burden of his prayer. From a vantage point on a hillside he could see his disciples struggling against the waves on the lake.

2 The Romans divided the time between sunset and sunrise into four watches. Jesus approached the boat walking on the water between 3 o'clock and 6 o'clock in the morning. His disciples thought that they were seeing a ghost and were terrified. Jesus spoke to reassure them, "Courage! It is I. Don't be afraid!". Peter wanted proof and asked if he could walk towards him on the water. The strong wind swept away any faith he had and he began to sink. Jesus grabbed him and said "What little faith you have! Why did you doubt?".

3 The climax of the story is not the stilling of the storm but the confession and worship of the disciples. They declare, "Truly you are the Son of God". This is the first time that they have addressed Jesus in this way. Quite what they meant by it is unclear. Probably they were seeing him as the Messiah (God's chosen messenger).

THE STORY

It had been a busy time for Jesus. He had just fed a large crowd of people using only five loaves and two fish. He needed some time to himself. He sent his disciples across to the other side of the lake in a boat. He climbed up a hill to spend some time praying to God, his Father. As darkness fell he could see his disciples struggling hard against the waves in the middle of the lake. They needed his help. He walked towards them on the water. As you can imagine, his disciples were very frightened by this. In fact, they were terrified. They thought that it was a ghost but Jesus told them not to be afraid. Peter asked Jesus if he could walk towards him on the water. Jesus told him to come. After one or two steps Peter began to sink. The wind was very strong. Jesus reached out to him and guided him back into the boat. Jesus told his disciples that they should have much more faith. This only frightened the disciples more. They fell down at the feet of Jesus and worshipped him.

DISCUSSION POINTS

1 *The Bible story of Jesus walking on water.*

2 *Jesus helping people.* What did the disciples need? What were they afraid of? How did Jesus offer them help? How might believing in Jesus help people today?

3 *Faith.* What does it mean? How do we show faith in our everyday lives? What does this faith mean? What did Jesus really want his disciples to do?

 NAME..

Jesus walking on the sea of Galilee

Read Matthew 15.22-33.
Rewrite the story in your own words, describing each of the following:

1. Jesus praying on the mountain.

2. Disciples rowing against the waves.

3. Peter sinking beneath the water.

4. Jesus reaching out to Peter.

Feeding a large crowd

AIMS

The aims of this section are to introduce:

1 The details of one of the most important miracles in the Gospels (the feeding of a large crowd)

2 The importance and meaning of the miracle.

KEY WORDS

Disciples

Eucharist

Gospels

Kingdom of God

Lake of Galilee

Matthew 6.1-15; Mark 6.30-44; Luke 9.10-17; John 6.1-15

1 Jesus sent out his twelve disciples to preach and on their return they withdrew, with him, to rest in the village of Bethsaida. But the crowds followed Jesus and he welcomed all who came. He told them about God's Kingdom and healed many who were needy.

2 As evening came the disciples suggested that the people be sent away into local villages to find food. Jesus threw the onus back on them to find enough food. They responded, "All we have are five loaves and two fish". Only John's account mentions a small boy providing these. Bread was the staple food and was often eaten with fish from the Lake of Galilee. We are told that Jesus took the bread, gave thanks to God and distributed it to the people. He did the same with the fish. Everyone had all that they needed.

3 This miracle is the only one recorded in all four Gospels (a clear indication of its importance in the Early Church). Scholars have suggested that this was because of the obvious links between this event and the celebration of the Eucharist by the early Christians.

THE STORY

Jesus and his disciples had been very busy and they were tired. They took themselves off to a lonely place to get their strength back but a large crowd followed them. In the end there were more than 5,000 people there but hardly anyone had brought any food with them. At the end of the day Jesus wanted to know just how much food they had between themselves. The disciples found a young boy who had five loaves and two fish but nobody else had any food. Jesus told his disciples to sit the people down in neat rows on the grass. He took the five loaves in his hands, gave God thanks for them and gave them to his disciples. They gave the bread out. There was more than enough to go round. Jesus then did the same with the fish. Again, there was more than enough for everyone to eat. At the end of the meal the disciples went round to collect up all the leftovers. They ended up with twelve full baskets – from just five loaves and two fish. This was one of the most famous miracles which Jesus carried out.

DISCUSSION POINTS

1 *The Bible story of the feeding of the five thousand.* If possible, have five loaves and two fish in your hands. Ask the children how many people they would expect these to feed. What do they think the miracle showed?

2 *Imagining the event.* Allow the children to imagine that they were present at the event. How would the boy in the story feel? How would the disciples feel as they gave the food out? How would people in the crowd feel?

The young boy and his food

Read John 6.1-13.

Jesus was with his disciples in a very lonely place. Soon, however, more than 5,000 people joined him there. When it grew late Jesus asked his disciples how much food they could find. The people were growing very hungry. They gathered together just five loaves and two fish. This was the food brought by a young boy. Jesus took this food and fed the whole crowd with it. They had so much to eat that 12 baskets of scraps were gathered up afterwards.

What do you think the young boy told his mother when he went home that evening? How do you think his mother replied?

The great catch of fish

AIMS

The aims of this section are to introduce:

1 One of the Gospel stories involving Jesus and his disciples after his resurrection

2 What the disciples did after Jesus died (many of them returned to fishing)

3 The part played by Peter in the story.

KEY WORDS

Ascension	Jerusalem
Disciples	John
Galilee	Peter
Gospels	Resurrection
James	Thomas

John 21.1-14

1 This is the third appearance that Jesus made to his disciples after his resurrection. It happened between the beginning of the second week after Jesus's crucifixion and the Ascension outside Jerusalem. The seven disciples to whom Jesus appeared included Simon Peter, Thomas, Nathaniel and the sons of Zebedee (James and John). They probably returned to Galilee to escape scrutiny by the mob in Jerusalem which had crucified Jesus.

2 Peter suggested that they spend the night fishing and the others agreed. It was fruitless. They caught nothing. Jesus appeared in the early morning just as the day was breaking. The disciples failed to recognise him and he asked them if they had caught anything. He told them to cast the net on the right hand side of the boat and they did so. The resulting catch was so great that they could not take the net into the boat. They recognised Jesus.

3 Grasping his outer cloak around him Peter dived overboard. The other disciples rowed to the shore and brought the net to land. A charcoal fire was already alight and they cooked some of the fish they had caught. Peter returned to the boat and brought the net ashore containing 153 fish. Jesus shared the meal with them.

THE STORY

Jesus had been put to death and had come back to life. But the disciples did not know this. When Jesus died they had returned to their old lives as fishermen. They put out to sea one night but caught nothing all night. Just as the dawn was breaking they saw someone standing on the shore. He called out to them and asked whether they had caught anything. They hadn't. The figure on the shore told them to drop their nets to the right of the boat. They did so and their nets were so full of fish they almost broke. One of the disciples recognised the person on the shore. It was Jesus. Peter was so excited he leapt overboard and went to Jesus. The others brought the boat to land. Jesus already had a fire burning on the sand. They cooked some of the fish they had caught and ate them with Jesus. It was a lovely meal.

DISCUSSION POINTS

1 *The Bible story of the great catch of fish.*

2 *Picnics.* What picnics have you had? Did you enjoy them? What makes a picnic special? Why was this picnic very special for the disciples?

See Factsheet 15, on page 24.

 NAME..

The fish

Read John 21.1-14.
Soon after Jesus had risen from the dead he appeared to his disciples.

They were fishing.

1. Peter said to some of the disciples …

2. The other disciples said to Peter …

3. Jesus told them to …

4. When they did so they …

5. Peter was excited and …

Being happy

AIMS

The aims of this section are to introduce:

1 The teaching of Jesus about happiness

2 The reverse of human values in God's kingdom.

KEY WORDS

Kingdom of Heaven

Matthew 5.3-12

1 This is the opening of the so-called 'Sermon on the Mount'. But it is highly unlikely that the teachings of Matthew 5-7 were ever delivered as a sermon. Rather, Matthew gathered together the teachings of Jesus on many topics which were delivered at various times during his ministry. In so doing he has provided us with the most important collection of that teaching in any of the Gospels.

2 The opening verses of this collection are called the Beatitudes (from the Latin word 'beatus', meaning 'happy'). They speak of the person who is favoured by God and so is truly happy. The full experience of this spiritual happiness will either be in this world or the next:

a. Those who are spiritually poor will enter God's Kingdom.
b. Those who mourn for their own sins, or for those of others, will be comforted by God.
c. Those who are humble will receive what God has promised them.
d. Those who do God's work will be fully satisfied.
e. Those who treat others with mercy will be treated in the same way by God.
f. Those who have a pure heart will see God.
g. Those who work for peace in this world will be called God's children.
h. Those who are persecuted and insulted by others will enter the kingdom of God.

THE STORY

Jesus spent a lot of his time on his own with his disciples. He wanted to teach them so many things about God. One day, sitting with them on the side of a hill, he told them what it means to be really happy. He surprised them with many of the things he said.

He told them that anyone who is sad will be happy because God will comfort them. The person who does not think they are important will be happy because God will give them real importance. Those people who put others first will be happy because God will put them first. The people who try to bring peace into the world will be happy because they are God's own children. Anyone who is persecuted, insulted by others or even killed will also be happy. God is keeping a very special reward for them in heaven.

DISCUSSION POINTS

1 *The Beatitudes.*

2 *Real happiness.* What is happiness? When have you been really happy? What did that happiness depend on? What did Jesus mean by happiness?

3 The different ways that Jesus and people today think of happiness. Does happiness depend on money?

Real happiness

Read Matthew 5.3-12.
Jesus taught his disciples many important things. Once, sitting on a hillside, he taught them about real happiness.

Fill in the missing words from these sentences:

1. Happy are the ______________ in ________ , they will see __________ .

2. Happy are those who are _______ _____________ they will receive what ___________ has ____________ .

3. Happy are those who _________ , ____________ will comfort them.

4. Happy are those who know that they are _________ _________ , the ___________ of _________ belongs to them.

5. Happy are those who are ___________ _____________ will be _____________ to them.

Some of the Beatitudes are missing from this list. Write them out in your best handwriting and decorate your page with a border.

Loving our enemies

AIMS

The aims of this section are to introduce:

1 The teachings of Jesus about seeking revenge

2 The teachings of Jesus about 'going the extra mile'

3 The teachings of Jesus about loving our enemies.

KEY WORDS

Old Testament

Matthew 5.38-48; Luke 6.27-36

1 The Old Testament approach to punishment was based on the principle of lex talionis (an eye for an eye and a tooth for a tooth). This did not condone revenge but it was the simplest way to punish the criminal. Jesus laid down a new principle. Not only was revenge not acceptable for his followers but, in addition, they should:

- offer their left cheek to those who slap them on the right
- give their coat to those who sue them for their shirt
- carry the pack of a Roman soldier twice the distance that the occupying army required
- give freely to those who wanted to borrow.

2 Jesus then turns to love, and the demands it makes. The old teaching encouraged love, but only towards one's own kind. Jesus wanted his followers to actively love those who hated them since even the tax collectors loved other tax collectors! Jesus wants his followers to follow an 'extraordinary' way of life. "You must be perfect," he said, "just as your Father in heaven is perfect" (Matthew 5.48). This way may not come naturally but it is God's way.

THE STORY

Jesus teaches his disciples that they should live very special kinds of lives. They must show other people that they really love them. They can do this in many different ways. If someone needs their shirt, they should give him their coat as well. If someone hits them on the right cheek they should turn their left one as well. If a Roman soldier forces them to carry his pack for one kilometre, they should offer to carry it twice as far.

For the disciples these things were hard enough but it wasn't all that Jesus was asking of them. Jesus went on. "Everyone loves his or her friends. That is easy. The really difficult thing is to love those whom we do not like." He encouraged his disciples to love their enemies.

"God will not reward those people who only love those who loved them first. Everyone does that. Even the tax-collectors, who cheat people out of their money, love other tax-collectors. God is perfect and he expects us to try to be as perfect as we can be."

DISCUSSION POINTS

1 *The teachings of Jesus about revenge and loving one's enemies.*

2 *The feelings we have when someone hurts us.* How do you feel if someone hits you or says something unkind? What goes through your mind? Do you want to get your own back? Why? What does Jesus suggest our response should be? Is that response possible?

3 *Do we only love people that we like?* Is it possible to love the people that we don't like, at least at first? How would this make our lives different? How would it make the world different?

 NAME...

Loving others

Read Matthew 5.38-48.

Jesus had some hard things to say to his disciples about loving others.

Draw and write about four things that Jesus told his disciples to do.

1.

2.

3.

4.

The Lord's Prayer

AIMS

The aims of this section are to introduce:

1 The general comments of Jesus about prayer

2 The prayer which Jesus taught his followers.

KEY WORDS

The Lord's Prayer

Fatherhood of God

Matthew 6.5-15; Luke 11.2-4

1 On more than one occasion, Jesus accused the religious leaders of hypocrisy. Here he attacks those who draw attention to themselves by praying ostentatiously in public, and those who deliberately use long words in their prayers to draw attention to themselves. In both ways, he said, they misunderstand the relationship between God and prayer. God cannot be impressed by what we say. He already knows what we need before we ask.

2 To help his followers, Jesus introduced the model prayer which he encouraged them to use ("This, then, is how you should pray ..."). The model prayer is based upon the Fatherhood of God (a designation for God that formed the foundation of Jesus's whole teaching). God is holy and he is setting up his kingdom (rule) on earth just as he has done in heaven. His followers have a crucial part to play in this. God shows how much he loves his followers by taking care of their everyday needs ("Give us today the food we need."). God offers forgiveness to all those who ask for it but Jesus suggests that whether we will be forgiven depends on our willingness to forgive others. Everyone is tempted but God can guarantee that such temptation will not be beyond our power to resist.

THE STORY

Jesus often prayed to God. He prayed to God before he had a big decision to make. He prayed to God after he had healed and taught crowds of people. He wanted his followers to learn to pray to God as well. What he didn't want them to do was to follow the example of some of those around them. Jesus disliked those who prayed in public, and used long words, so that other people would think they were holy.

Jesus told his followers how they should pray. To begin with they should pray in secret, on their own. Then they should use the prayer that Jesus gave them. (We know this as 'the Lord's Prayer' and you have probably said/heard it many times.) It begins with 'Our Father'. (Jesus often called God 'Father'.) In this prayer we ask God, Our Father, to give us the bread that we need each day. We should also ask him to forgive us our sins. God promises to forgive our sins if we forgive other people for what they have done wrong. (You cannot be forgiven by God if you do not forgive others.) God will also keep us safe if we trust him.

DISCUSSION POINTS

1 *The Lord's Prayer.*

2 *The religious practices that Jesus did not like.* Why did Jesus object to praying in public and using long words? Why should people want to impress others in this way? What did Jesus himself suggest they do instead?

3 *Why do people use the Lord's Prayer?* When is it used? What does it say?

 NAME...

Our Father

As a class or in groups, work out a way of putting the Lord's Prayer into modern English.

Our Father in heaven

May your holy name be honoured

May your Kingdom come

May your will be done on earth as it is in heaven

Give us today the food we need

Forgive us the wrongs we have done

as we forgive the wrongs that others have done to us

Do not bring us to hard testing

but keep us safe from the Evil One.

The sower

AIMS

The aims of this section are to introduce:

1 One of the most important parables told by Jesus (the parable of the sower)

2 The different kinds of soil mentioned in the story (and the explanation).

KEY WORDS

Good Soil

Matthew 13.1-9; 18-23

1 This was thought by the Early Church to be a very important parable. The focus of the parable is not on the sower or the seed but on the different kinds of soil on to which the seed falls:

a. Some seed falls on the paths which run through and around the unfenced land and is promptly eaten by the birds.
b. Some falls on very shallow earth where the limestone bedrock is very close to the surface. This is scorched by the sun as soon as the rainy season ends.
c. Some falls into thorn hedges that deprive it of nourishment.
d. Some falls into good soil and grows.

2 An explanation of the parable is added although this is unique and so unlikely to have come from Jesus, as he left his listeners to apply his parables to themselves. In the explanation given, the seed is the message of Jesus which receives a varied welcome. Some hear the truth but do not allow it to penetrate beyond the surface. Some receive the message enthusiastically but when persecution appears they give up. Others choke the message with their own worries and cares. The good soil symbolises those who welcome God's Kingdom and become followers.

THE STORY

One day, Jesus went down to the lakeside and began to teach the people. So many came to listen to him that he climbed into a boat and pushed off from the shore. He told the people a story from the boat. A farmer went out to sow his seed. As he walked along he threw the seed to the right and to the left. This was a very wasteful way of sowing seed. Some fell on the path where the birds swooped down to gobble it up. Some fell on rocky ground where the hot sun soon scorched it. Some fell amongst thorn bushes which choked the seed almost before it landed. But some fell on to good ground and produced some very good corn for the farmer.

Jesus wasn't finished yet. He told the people that the different kinds of soil were just like the people who listened to what he had to say. In some people his message never took root. Others began to listen but their interest did not last very long. Some welcomed what Jesus had to say until the worries and cares of their lives killed his teaching. There were some, however, who took his message seriously and they became his followers. Jesus was very happy with them.

DISCUSSION POINTS

1 *The Bible story of the sower and the different kinds of soil.*

2 *The way that seed was sown then and now.* What are the differences? Which is the most effective method? Why? Was the farmer happy to lose so much of his seed?

3 *Responses to the story.* As they listen to the story of Jesus are they disinterested or apathetic? Is there an initial interest which soon ends? Is there great interest? Why do people respond differently? (Children in your class will have various religions and beliefs and you will need to use your sensitivity and judgement in taking account of this.)

4 *The seed that falls on to good soil.* Talk about the 'good soil' as a person. What is this person like?

 NAME...

The sower and his seed

Read Matthew 13.1-9.

1. Complete the sentences using the words below.

A farmer went to _______ seeds in his field. He walked up and down sowing ____________ everywhere. Some of the seed fell on the ___________ and were eaten by ____________ . Some seed fell on ______ ______ where the _______ was not very deep. The sun dried the young plants up. Some seed fell among ________ bushes. The plants were __________ by the thorns. Some seed fell in ___________ soil. Here the plants grew __________ and were healthy.

seeds	rocky ground	path	strong	thorn
sow	choked	good	soil	birds

2. Circle the correct answer in each sentence below. Then copy the sentence into your book.

a. For Christians, the seed that fell on the path is like the person who cares/does not care about the teaching of Jesus.

b. For Christians, the seed that fell on rocky ground is like the person who stays with Jesus/soon gives up on Jesus.

c. For Christians, the seed that fell among thorns is like the person who is too busy/never too busy for Jesus.

d. For Christians, the seed that falls on to good ground is like the person who believes/does not believe in Jesus and his teaching.

The lost sheep

AIMS

The aims of this section are to introduce:

1 The parable of the lost sheep

2 The meaning of the parable and the celebrations that take place when the lost sheep is found.

KEY WORDS

Parable

Pharisees

Teachers of the Law

Matthew 18.12-14; Luke 15.1-7

This parable in Luke is the first of three stories linked together by the common theme of being lost. The lost sheep is followed by the lost coin and the lost son.

1 The situation described by Jesus in the parable was a common one in first century Palestine. A normal sized flock consisted of one hundred sheep which were entrusted to the care of one shepherd. A conscientious shepherd would count his sheep each night to make sure that none were missing. Often sheep were left in the open country if there was not a sheep enclosure nearby.

2 Two things are striking about this parable. First, there is the obvious analogy between the shepherd looking for the lost sheep and Jesus seeking out lost people (outsiders). This analogy is one of Luke's most common themes. Secondly, the climax of the story is not just the return of the sheep but the triumphant note in its discovery. The shepherd places it across his shoulders, calling to his friends and neighbours to join him in the celebration. Jesus is stressing, both in the parable and also by direct statement, that his work of rescuing the lost is pleasing to God.

THE STORY

This is a story told by Jesus. You might know it already. Jesus spent a lot of time with people that others did not want to know. The religious leaders of his community were grumbling about the company that he kept so Jesus decided to tell this story. As he told the story he may well have seen a flock of sheep on the hillside. Each flock had its own shepherd. This shepherd looked after his sheep and made sure that they were safe.

One night, a shepherd counted his flock before settling down to sleep and found that one sheep was missing. "What," Jesus asked, "would you expect the shepherd to do?". Jesus said that the shepherd would make sure that his sheep were safe and then he would set off to find the missing one. When he found the missing sheep he would place it across his shoulders and carry it back to join the other sheep. He would be so happy. When he arrived back he would call to all his friends and neighbours to join him in the celebration.

Jesus said that he was just like the shepherd. God sent him to find those people who had lost their way. When he finds one lost person, he brings them into God's Kingdom. God is so happy every time this happens.

DISCUSSION POINTS

1 *The Bible story of the lost sheep.*

2 *Sheep.* What do you know about sheep? What are their characteristics? Do they have a tendency to get themselves into awkward situations? What is the importance of the flock staying together? (Talk about sheep-dog trials, etc.) Can you find any similarities between sheep and humans?

 NAME...

Finding the sheep

You are a shepherd and you have lost your sheep. Can you find it? Trace the route you need to take to find the missing sheep.

The lost coin

AIMS

The aims of this section are to introduce:

1 The short parable of the lost coin

2 The links between the parable of the lost coin and the parables of the lost sheep and the lost son

3 The link between this parable and the parable of the sinner who asks God to forgive him.

KEY WORDS

Angel

Parable

Luke 15.8-10

1 The coins which the woman lost in this parable were 'drachmas' and each one was worth about a day's wages. The mention of the ten coins at the outset of the story implies that this was all that the woman had. The woman lights a lamp to search for the missing coin because her house had only a few, small window spaces and a low doorway. She sweeps the hard, earthen floor of her house to locate the coin by its clinking sound. As she almost certainly lived in a single-room house there would be only a few places that the coin could have been.

2 The celebration when the coin is found parallels that when the lost sheep is located by its shepherd in the earlier parable. The rejoicing may seem a little exaggerated but becomes understandable when we remember the neighbourly spirit often found in small communities. It must also be remembered that this coin represented ten per cent of the woman's savings. The final comment of Jesus reinforces this. As we have already discovered in Luke 15.7, there is enormous joy in heaven over just one sinner who repents.

THE STORY

Do you remember the story that Jesus told about a lost sheep which was found by the shepherd? Jesus also told another story which was similar. But this time it was a coin, rather than a sheep, that was lost.

A woman had ten coins. Coins were called 'drachmas' in the time of Jesus. You had to do a whole day's work if you wanted to earn one drachma in those days.

Well, this woman lost one of her coins. As she only had ten of them to begin with she was very upset by this. She lived in a house with only one room so it should not have been too difficult to find the missing coin. First she lit her lamp, because the room was very dark. Then she swept every nook and cranny of the house because she knew that if she swept the coin up she would hear it clinking. She must have found her coin by sweeping the floor although Jesus does not tell us just where and how she found it in the end.

The first thing the woman did when she found the coin was to call all her neighbours in. They celebrated together. Jesus told those listening that God is just as happy as this when someone is sorry for their sins. The angels of God celebrate together.

DISCUSSION POINTS

1 *The Bible story of the missing coin.*

2 *Things which are lost.* Have you ever lost anything that was special to you? Where did you look for it? Did you find it? Were you very glad if you found it? Why was the woman in the story particularly glad?

See Factsheet 10, page 19.

COPYMASTER 48 NAME..

Finding the coin

Jesus told a story about a woman who had ten coins. She lost one of them in her house and she was very upset. Can you help her find it?

Draw a circle round the coin when you have found it.

What did the woman do when she had found the coin?

____

____

____

____

____

____

____

The lost son

AIMS

The aims of this section are to introduce:

1 The third of the 'lost' parables in Luke 15 (that of the lost/prodigal son)

2 The love of the father for his wayward son

3 The welcome home given to the son by his father.

KEY WORDS

Prodigal Son

Luke 15.11-24

1 In the Jewish tradition, a younger son was given one-third of his father's inheritance and the older son two-thirds. Although the inheritance was usually allocated when the father died it could be divided earlier if everyone agreed.

2 As all contact with pigs was strictly forbidden in the religious laws, no Jewish person would consider feeding them for a living. To do so would mean surrendering one's Jewish identity. In the story, the son's occupation is a sign of how far he had fallen. The pods which he ended up eating came from the carob tree. This food was reserved for animals and the very poor.

3 It was a combination of his hunger and sorrow for his past life that compelled the son to return home. The welcome that he received from his father was totally unexpected. His father saw him coming from a distance and welcomed him warmly. The prize calf was killed and a robe was placed around the son's shoulders, a ring put on his finger and shoes on his feet. As with the other two parables, the discovery of that which was lost ended with a celebration. Although Jesus did not say so, his listeners would not have missed the clear parallel between the behaviour of the father in the story and that of God who welcomes the lost sinner with similar warmth.

THE STORY

Today we are going to listen to one of the most well known stories of Jesus. There was once a wealthy man who had two sons. One day the younger son approached his father and asked for the money which would come to him when his father died. He left home with the money but soon wasted it all. He became penniless. The only job he could find was feeding pigs. This upset him a lot. (He was Jewish and Jewish people were not allowed to have anything to do with pigs.) It was when he ended up so poor he had to eat the food meant for the pigs that he decided to swallow his pride and go home to his father.

He did not know how his father would welcome him. As it happened his father was looking out for him. As soon as he saw his son coming he ran to him. He put his arms around his son. He told a servant to kill the prize bull so that everyone could have a feast. A new cloak was put around the son's shoulders. A ring was placed on his finger. A new pair of sandals were put on his feet. Everyone had a wonderful time.

DISCUSSION POINTS

1 *The Bible story of the prodigal son.*

2 *The feelings of the younger son.* Imagine each person into the shoes of the younger son. Why did you want to leave home? Did your father give in too easily? What did your father give you? Did you waste the money? How do you think your older brother feels now?

3 *The reaction of the father.* Was the father's reaction surprising? Why was he watching out for his son? What did he do when he saw his son coming? How do you think he felt?

 NAME...

The son returns

Read Luke 15.11-24.

You will find the answers to all of these questions in the story.

1. Who lived in the family home?

2. What did the younger son want to do?

3. What did his father give him?

4. How did the younger son spend his money?

5. What happened when the money ran out?

6. What decision did the son make?

7. How did the father receive his son?

8. What happened at the end of the story?

The houses on rock and sand

AIMS

The aims of this section are to introduce:

1 The story about the two builders who built their houses on different foundations

2 The different ways that people responded to Jesus and his teaching.

KEY WORDS

Good Foundations

Matthew 7.24-27

1 In this parable the two houses looked equally safe in the good weather. But Palestine is known for its torrential rains that can turn dry wadis (the dry beds of torrents) into raging torrents. Only a storm could reveal the real difference between the work of the two builders. The point being made is that the wise builder constructs his house to withstand anything that the elements throw at it.

2 In the story, the wise person is the man or woman who puts the teachings of Jesus into practice. They are building their lives to withstand anything thrown at them. Those who pretend to have faith are foolish builders. When the storms of life come they turn out to have built on the wrong foundations, depending on their own rather than God's wisdom.

THE STORY

Jesus once told a story about two men who each built a house. One of them built a house on rock and the other built it on sand. As long as the weather stayed fine then both buildings stood up. But Palestine saw some very heavy rain from time to time. When storms blew up some houses were always badly damaged. The house built on the rock could withstand anything because it was built on a solid foundation. The foundation of the house built on the sand, however, was very soft. As the rain came down so the sand shifted and, before long, the house came tumbling down.

Who do you think was the wisest of the two men? Obviously the man who built his house on the rock was the wisest. Jesus wanted his listeners to learn a very important lesson from this. Some people listening to him became followers. They were like the man who built on the rock. When the storms blew in their lives they did not crumble underneath them. Jesus taught that those who did not build their lives on the right values were just like the man who built his house on the sand. They had no firm foundations.

DISCUSSION POINTS

1 *The Bible story of the two house-builders.*

2 *The importance of a house's foundations.* Why do foundations matter? What happens if they are not secure? (Give examples such as houses falling into the sea, etc.) What was the difference between the two houses in the story? What was the outcome?

 NAME...

The two houses

Read Matthew 7.24-27.

Jesus told a story about two houses. They looked exactly the same from the outside. When a storm blew up, however, there was one very important difference:

In the fine weather …

When the storm blew …

The lesson that Jesus was teaching was …

The Good Samaritan

AIMS

The aims of this section are to introduce:

1 The story of the Good Samaritan

2 The enmity between Jewish people and the Samaritans at that time

3 The kindness shown by the Samaritan traveller.

KEY WORDS

Dead Sea	Parable
Jericho	Priest
Jerusalem	Samaritan
Jew	Temple
Levite	

Luke 10.25-37

1 It was about seventeen miles from Jerusalem to Jericho and the road descended sharply towards the River Jordan, just north of the Dead Sea. The rocky, rugged terrain provided good cover for robbers and this made the journey particularly dangerous.

2 The story of the Good Samaritan is told by Jesus in response to the lawyer's question, 'Who is my neighbour?'. The lawyer would have expected to be told by Jesus that his neighbour was any Jewish person but this was not the answer Jesus gave. In placing a Samaritan at the heart of his story he was drawing attention to a deep animosity between Jews and Samaritans which went back over three hundred years. There was minimal contact between the two groups. A priest and a Levite (an official in the Temple) passed the injured man by but in the story it was the Samaritan who responded to simple human need.

THE STORY

Jesus often told stories, or parables, to help people to understand what God wanted them to do. One day a person came to ask Jesus a question. He knew that, as a Jew, he was expected to love his neighbour but he wasn't quite sure just what this meant. In the story that Jesus told him, a Jewish man set off to travel between the towns of Jerusalem and Jericho, a distance of seventeen miles. The journey was dangerous because robbers often hid among the rocks to jump out on travellers. On this journey the Jewish man was beaten up and robbed. He was seriously hurt and needed help quickly. A Jewish priest and another man (a Levite) came walking along the road but they were both too frightened to help. Then a third man came along. The third man was a Samaritan. The Jews and the Samaritans had been enemies for hundreds of years. But the Samaritan stopped and put the injured man on his donkey. He led the donkey to the nearest inn. He asked the inn-keeper to look after the man until he returned that way. He left some money to pay for the injured man's food and medicine.

DISCUSSION POINTS

1 *The Bible story of the Good Samaritan.* Tell, read or dramatise the story.

2 *Those people in society who are in need now.* What kind of help do these people need?

3 *When we need help.* Discuss, drawing on the experience of the children, ways in which they need help. When have you recently needed help? What about parents, grandparents, friends, neighbours, etc.? What help did they need? Who helped them? Discuss the role of the Samaritan's helpline. Can you find out/guess why they're called The Samaritans?

The Good Samaritan helps

Read Luke 10.25-37.

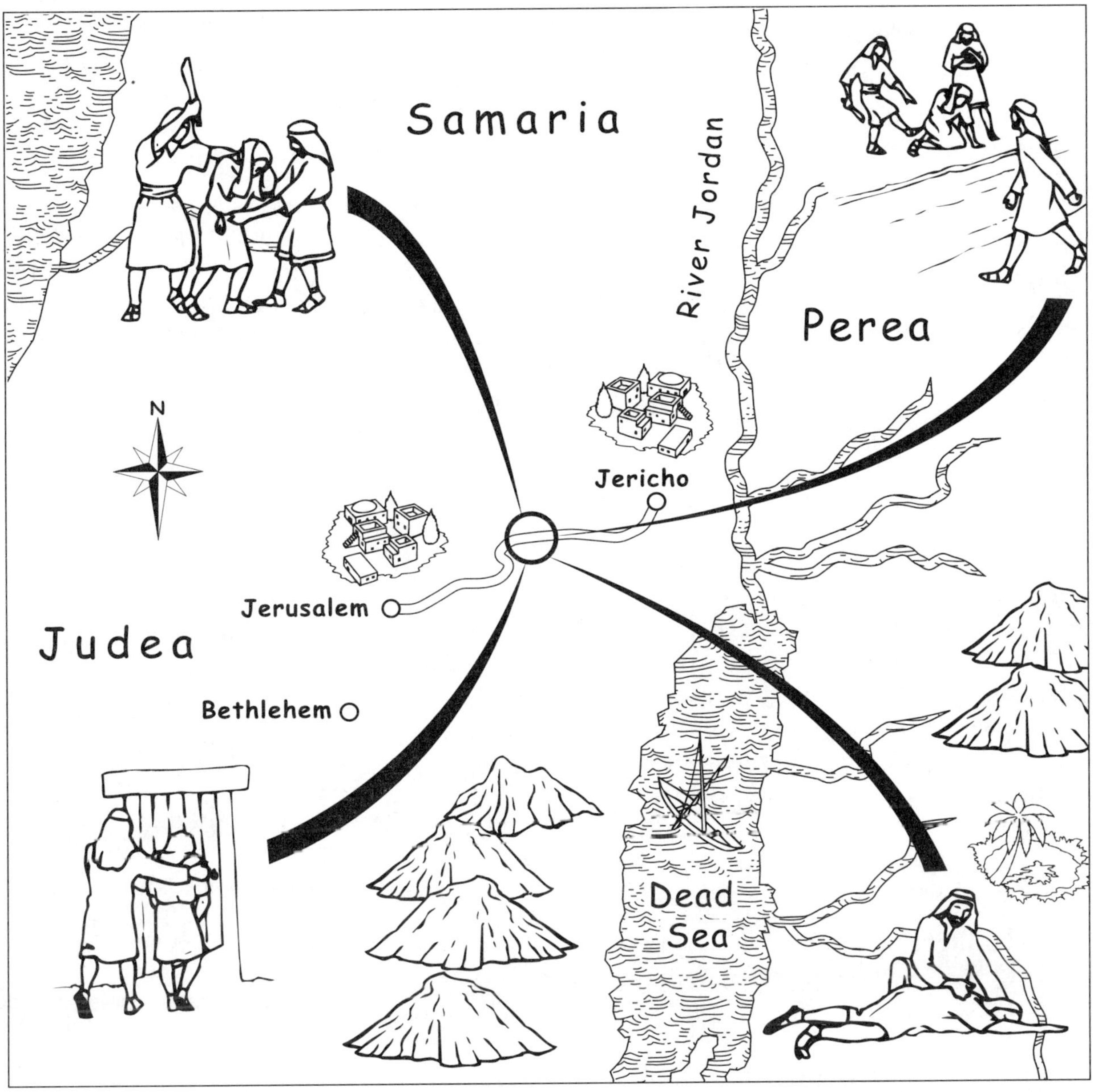

Fill in the missing words from those listed at the bottom:

A man was travelling between ____________ and ________ . He was attacked by ___________ who left him injured by the side of the _______. Two men, a ________ and a__________ passed by on the other side. A _______ picked him up and laid him across his __________ . He took the man to the nearest ________ and told the ___________to look after him until he was well.

robbers	*inn-keeper*	*Jericho*	*road*	*inn*
priest	*Jerusalem*	*Levite*	*donkey*	*Samaritan*

The Pharisee and the tax-collector

AIMS

The aims of this section are to introduce:

1 The story of two men praying in the Temple

2 The meaning and importance of humility.

KEY WORDS

Disciple	Parable
Gospel	Pharisee
Jerusalem	Temple
Luke	

Luke 18.9-14

1 The Pharisees were the group of religious leaders who, according to the Gospels, led the opposition to Jesus. Here they are cast as leading players in one of the parables of Jesus. They are taken to symbolise the attitude of pride and self-vindication which upset Jesus so much. The Pharisee follows the custom of standing whilst praying in the Temple. His prayer expresses the essence of being a Pharisee (separation from others).

2 The opposing attitude towards God is expressed by the tax-collector. He crops up more than once in Luke's Gospel to represent those who were social outcasts. His activity as the collector of taxes for the occupying Roman army made sure that he was separated socially and religiously from all orthodox Jewish believers. But his prayer is totally unpretentious and wins the favour of God. As with almost all parables of Jesus the most important comment is reserved until the end, "all who make themselves great will be humbled and all who humble themselves will be made great".

THE STORY

The Temple stood in the middle of the city of Jerusalem. It was very large and many people went there every day to pray. One day Jesus was standing in one of the Temple's courtyards with his disciples when they saw an important looking man start to pray. He made sure that everyone saw him as he told God that he was glad that he was not like other people. He was much more important and religious than they were. Jesus told his disciples that God was not very impressed with this man.

Then a very different man started to pray. He had very few friends because he worked for the Romans. (He collected taxes from Jewish people for the Romans.) This made him very unpopular indeed. And when he prayed he would not even look up to heaven. Instead, he looked at the ground and simply asked God to forgive him for his sins. Jesus said that God was very pleased with the prayer of this man. He left those listening to him to work out just why.

DISCUSSION POINTS

1 *The Bible story of the Pharisee and the tax-collector.*

2 *The two people in the Temple praying.* Encourage the children to imagine the two people praying. What do you see? How are the two people dressed? What are they doing? What is the difference between their actions?

See Factsheets 5 and 6, pages 14 and 15.

 NAME..

Two men praying

Read Luke 18.10-14.

As you know, Jesus told many parables (stories). In one of them two men went into the Temple to pray. The men were very different and so were their prayers. Write those prayers out, in your own words, and draw pictures to go with them.

Complete the following sentences on a separate page.

God was not pleased with the prayer of the religious man because …

God was pleased with the prayer of the tax-collector because …

The caller at midnight

AIMS

The aims of this section are to introduce:

1 The parable of the man in need who calls on his friend at midnight

2 How Jesus linked the parable with prayer.

KEY WORDS

Luke

Gospel

Holy Spirit

Parable

Matthew 26.69-75; Mark 14. 66-72; Luke 22.56-62; John 18.15-18; 25-27

1 This parable is only found in Luke's Gospel. The scene of the story is a Palestinian house in which all the members of the family are asleep in the only room (and probably all on the same mat). The father cannot climb over everyone to reach the door without disturbing them. In such a situation nobody will be happy to respond to a knock at the door, especially in the middle of the night. Nevertheless the unwritten rules of Eastern hospitality demand that a response is made.

2 The point of the parable seems to be that if you are bold enough to keep asking your need will be met. In the parable, the man's boldness and persistence finally wear down his friend. But unlike the father in the story, God is always waiting to graciously answer the prayers of those people who recognise their need and ask. If even bad people know how to give good things to their children then how much more readily will God give the Holy Spirit to those people who ask. God is perfect and the gifts that he gives are also perfect.

THE STORY

Jesus often took his stories from real life. One story that he told would have raised a smile or two from his listeners. They, too, would have lived in one-roomed houses where, at night, everyone slept on the floor. They would not only share the same floor with the rest of the family but the same mat as well. When everyone settled down for the night there was no room for anyone to move around.

One night, a family was asleep. It was midnight. Suddenly there was a knock at the door and it woke the father up. It was a friend of the family. Someone had visited him late at night and he had no food to give his visitor. Could he borrow some? The father did not know what to do. Should he get up, speak with his friend and wake the whole family up? He thought about it carefully. He decided to meet his friend's needs because, if he kept knocking, he would wake everyone up anyway.

Jesus wanted his listeners to learn something important from the story. If human beings help others in need how much more will God help those who ask him? He is waiting to give them many good things. All that they need to do is to ask and keep on asking.

DISCUSSION POINTS

1 *The Bible story of the caller at midnight.*

2 *The father in the story.* Children can imagine that they are the father. How would you feel being woken up late at night? Would you be annoyed? Frightened? Would you want your whole family to be woken up? What would you say to your friend? Would you help him? If so, why?

See Factsheet 10, page 19.

 NAME...

A knock at the door

Read Luke 11.5-13.

Read the story of the friend who calls at midnight. Eastern people went to bed when it grew dark so at midnight everyone would be fast asleep. Imagine that you are the father in this story. You, and all your family, are fast asleep. Suddenly there is a knocking at the door.

Tell the story in four drawings.

What did Jesus say the story means?

The workers in the vineyard

AIMS

The aims of this section are to introduce:

1 The parable of Jesus about workers being hired to work in a vineyard

2 The 'fairness' of the landowner's actions.

KEY WORDS

Denarius

Parable

Matthew 20.1-16

1 The normal working day in the time of Jesus was about ten hours long and the landowner in the parable hired his first workers around six o'clock in the morning. He agreed to pay each of them one denarius (the normal wage paid to a soldier or a labourer) for a full day's work. A second group of workers were hired at nine o'clock in the morning. Those hired at this time were promised 'whatever is right'. A third group were standing around until much later in the day because nobody had hired them.

2 Labourers were paid at the end of each day. The foreman was told to pay them all the agreed wage and this he did in the story. The dispute arose because the workers are all paid the same wage whatever the length of their working day had been. The landowner responds that he has not cheated anyone. They have all been paid the agreed amount. As long as he has been just in his dealings with the workers, does he not have the right to do as he wishes with his own money? The point that Jesus is making is that God's gifts are not earned but are freely given. In God's Kingdom the driving force is not merit or ability but God's goodness.

THE STORY

In any Palestinian town, early in the morning, you would see men waiting around in the market square. They were a common sight. They waited because they were hoping to be hired for a day's work. Jesus used these men in one of his stories.

A landowner wanted to hire many men for the day. At six o'clock in the morning he found a group and hired them. They agreed to work for ten hours and to receive a denarius as wages. Three hours later the landowner needed some more workers and hired another group. He also paid them a denarius, even though they did not have to work for so long. Much later he needed some extra help and hired a third group. They did not work for very long at all but each one of them was also paid a denarius.

At the end of the day the men were given their wages (a denarius each). The men who had worked for ten hours thought that this was unfair. They said so. The landlord was very upset. "It is my money," he told those who were complaining, "I will do as I like with it". You might think the landowner was being unfair but Jesus told this story to teach everyone that God gave all of his gifts freely. Nobody earned them. Nobody could complain that God was unfair. In fact, in God's world, as Jesus said, the first are often last and the last first. What do you think he meant by that?

DISCUSSION POINTS

1 *The Bible story of the landlord and the workers.*

2 *Fairness.* Was the landowner being unfair? Were the workers right to complain? What was Jesus trying to teach about God?

 NAME..

The workers

Read Matthew 20.1-16.

Read this story for yourself and answer the following questions.

1. Why do you think the men who had worked since 6 o'clock were unhappy?

2. Do you think the other workers were happy with their money?

3. What did the landowner say to the men who were complaining?

4. What did Jesus want to teach in this parable?

The mustard seed and the yeast

AIMS

The aims of this section are to introduce:

1 The two tiny parables of Jesus (the mustard seed and the yeast)

2 The meaning of these parables.

KEY WORDS

Kingdom of God

Palestine

Parable

Matthew 13.31-33

1 In first century Palestine the mustard seed was the smallest of all seeds yet, once planted, it grew into a large tree. When Jesus told this parable, it would have recalled, for his Jewish listeners, passages in the Jewish Scriptures in which God's Kingdom was depicted as a large tree in whose branches birds lodged and built their nests. The point that Jesus was making was that his work and ministry was only making a small beginning. After his death his message about the kingdom of God would expand rapidly. The tiny seed now being planted would grow into a very large tree indeed.

2 The very brief parable of the yeast makes exactly the same point as the parable of the mustard seed. The beginnings of God's Kingdom on earth, with Jesus, are almost inconsequential. Not that yeast grows. It doesn't. It permeates. But the end result is the same. The tiniest amount of yeast mixed with forty litres of flour turns into dough that rises. In Jesus the Kingdom of God had just a small beginning. But Jesus was seeing into the future when its influence would be felt everywhere.

THE STORY

Sometimes Jesus told very short stories. If you had not been paying full attention to them you would have missed them altogether. Here are two of those stories. The first is about a very small mustard seed. There is no smaller seed anywhere than a mustard seed. A man takes one of these seeds and sows it in his field. For a while it seems that nothing is happening to it but it is growing beneath the surface of the soil. Then it pushes its way above the surface and keeps growing. Wait long enough and it will grow into a big tree. The branches will be so big that birds will be able to build their nests in its branches.

The second story is even shorter. If you want to turn flour into dough for bread you need one very important ingredient. That is yeast. Forget to put the yeast in and the dough would not rise.

What was Jesus saying in these two stories? Jesus had come to earth to tell people about God. Some had become disciples and followers but many hadn't. What Jesus was trying to do had only begun very slowly. It was like the mustard seed. Later, though, it would grow much larger. People all over the world would believe what Jesus had taught them.

DISCUSSION POINTS

1 *The Bible story of the mustard seed and yeast.*

2 *Gardening.* What happens when a seed is planted? How long before something appears above the ground? What happens if we grow impatient and dig it up? How do Christians today tell people about Jesus?

NAME...

Two tiny parables

Read Matthew 13.31-33.

Jesus came to earth to tell people about God's Kingdom. Those who believed in Jesus joined this kingdom. At first, the number of those who believed was very small. But God's Kingdom grew much larger. Jesus told two parables to show this. You can describe them below.

Parable 1

____

____

____

____

____

____

____

Parable 2

____

____

____

____

____

____

____

What was Jesus teaching in these two parables?

____

____

____

The treasure and the pearl

AIMS

The aims of this section are to introduce:

1 The parable of the hidden treasure

2 The parable of the pearl.

KEY WORDS

Kingdom of God

Parable

Matthew 13.44-46

1 The parable of the treasure hidden in a field and that of the pearl belong together and make the same teaching point. At the same time they have individual emphases. They both deal with the worth of the kingdom that Jesus is building. This kingdom is like treasure which is hidden in a field. Someone finds it by chance. Under Jewish law if a workman found treasure in a field and lifted it out it would belong to his master (the field's owner). But in the parable, the man is careful. He doesn't remove the treasure from the ground until he has bought the field. This shows how valuable the treasure is. It also shows the value of God's Kingdom (it is worth every sacrifice).

2 In the second parable there is a merchant whose business it is to seek out pearls. By chance he comes upon one which is supremely valuable. The pearl is so valuable that he sells everything he has to buy it. Jesus is saying that when a person hears his message about God's Kingdom it is worth making every possible sacrifice to own it.

THE STORY

Here are two very short stories that Jesus told. He wanted everyone to know that he had come to do God's work. He was setting up a kind of kingdom of God on earth. Everyone and anyone could join it but many were choosing not to. He believed they were making a great mistake. He said they were like a man who was digging a field and came across buried treasure. If they dug the treasure up there and then it would belong to their master. If they were wise they would cover the treasure up again, and then go and sell everything so that they could buy the field. The treasure is worth every penny they have to spend to buy the field.

Do you want to hear another story that teaches the same lesson? There was a man who spent his life searching for pearls. One day he found the most beautiful pearl in the world. It was so beautiful that he sold everything to be able to buy it.

Finding God's Kingdom is like digging up a treasure or finding a pearl beyond price. It is worth sacrificing everything to join God's Kingdom.

DISCUSSION POINTS

1 *The Bible stories, told by Jesus, about the hidden treasure and the pearl.*

2 *Stories that have a message/moral.* Tell some such stories. Discuss the meanings of these stories. Talk about the two parables. What was Jesus trying to teach people about God through them? What is the most important message of these two parables?

 NAME...

Find the hidden treasure

Read Matthew 13.44-46.

Jesus told a story about a man who discovered hidden treasure in a field. Try to find the path to the hidden treasure on the map below. Then draw in the box below what you think might be hidden in the treasure chest.

The two sons

AIMS

The aims of this section are to introduce:

1 The parable of the two sons

2 The importance of obeying God.

KEY WORDS

Kingdom of God

Parable

Matthew 21.28-32

1 This story is very straightforward. In it Jesus is teaching of those people who will enter the Kingdom of God and those who, through stubbornness, will not. He tells the story of two sons. A father tells his elder son to work in his vineyard but the son refuses to go. Later the son changes his mind and goes to work. The father also speaks to the younger son who promises to go but does not turn up for work. In the end, Jesus wonders, who really does what the father wants? Is the promise more important than the obedient action?

2 What Jesus is saying would have been shocking for his contemporaries but we can only fully appreciate just how much so when we understand the low esteem in which tax-collectors and prostitutes were held in Palestinian society. Jesus is saying that the social outcastes who began by denying God are now responding to the message of Jesus. They are doing what God demands of them and entering His kingdom. The religious people, on the other hand, claim to be obeying God but they do not listen to the message of Jesus. They will not be entering the Kingdom of God.

THE STORY

Jesus was very concerned to talk about God with everyone. But he found that many religious people did not think that they had to listen to what he was saying. They thought that they were in God's Kingdom already. On the other hand, those people that society looked down on were listening to what Jesus had to say about God. Jesus told a short story to explain his point.

A man had two sons and he wanted them both to spend the day working in his vineyard. He told his younger son to start work and the son said that he would. When his father's back was turned, however, the son took the day off. The man told his older son to start work but the son refused. But a little later he changed his mind and went to work. Jesus wanted to know which of his sons pleased his father most. What would your answer be? Jesus was in no doubt. The older son who changed his mind and went to work.

Jesus was making a very important point. There were people who listened to Jesus, said that they were interested and then did nothing about it. They were not likely to please God very much. God was much more pleased with those who were not interested to begin with but who thought about it and then decided that they wanted to follow Jesus. Some of the people who behaved like this were very unpopular with other people but they were popular with God.

DISCUSSION POINTS

1 *The Bible story of the two sons.*

2 *Place the choices facing these two sons in a modern family situation.* One person is told to do something by a parent, says they will and then does nothing about it. The other says that they will do nothing and then does it. Who is likely to please their parent most? Why?

Doing as you are told

Mr. and Mrs. Jones have two children. One, John, is eight years old. The other, Anne, is nine. In the picture, Mrs. Jones tells John to do something and Mr. Jones tells Anne to do something else. Can you guess what each one has just been told to do? What is John thinking? What is Anne thinking? What is Mrs. Jones thinking? What is Mr. Jones thinking? Look at the questions below and write your answers on a separate piece of paper.

Can you guess what Mrs. Jones told John to do? (Write your answer in the speech bubble.)

Do you think John will do as he was told?

What do you think will happen next?

Can you guess what Mr. Jones told Anne to do? (Write your answer in the speech bubble.)

Do you think Anne will do as she was told?

What do you think will happen next?

The growing seed

AIMS

The aims of this section are to introduce:

1 The Kingdom of God which Jesus came to build

2 The meaning of the 'seed' in the parable

3 The secret and mysterious growth of the seed.

KEY WORDS

Kingdom of God

Mark 4.26-29

1 Most of the parables of Jesus were concerned with the growth of the Kingdom (rule) of God on earth. Jesus came to bring a new message to the people. Those who responded to this message became members of God's Kingdom. The first members of this Kingdom were surprising (the tax-collectors, prostitutes and other outsiders).

2 Often the preaching of Jesus about this Kingdom is likened, as in the story, to seed growing in the ground. Once sown its early growth is beneath the ground where nobody can see it. The farmer's responsibility is to prepare the ground and sow the seed. He cannot make sure that the seed grows nor does he understand just how it happens. Its growth, and fruitfulness, is due to powers beyond his control. The Kingdom of God is growing on earth in a similar way. The responsibility of followers of Jesus is to show, by the lives they lead, that they have responded to his message. God is working in others to bring about a similar response. Some of them will believe but the responsibility for that lies with God not with the followers of Jesus.

THE STORY

When Jesus wanted to teach his listeners an important lesson he often spoke about things from everyday life. Many of his listeners were farmers. They knew that it was hard work to get the ground ready for sowing the seed each year. The earth needed to be broken up and made ready. Then the farmer walked up and down the land throwing his seed to the right and to the left. Much of the seed was wasted. But some seed did fall on the ground which had been specially prepared.

Beneath the earth amazing things happened to the seed. As it grew up to the surface of the earth it also began to grow roots down into the earth. This took some time. Each year the farmer wondered whether he would have a good crop. He did not know what was going on beneath the surface of the earth. He trusted the earth to give him a good crop. You can imagine his excitement when the plant broke through the surface and began to grow. The farmer looked at it every day. The tender stalk grew stronger and stronger. The ear of the corn appeared and this filled up with corn. Finally the big day arrived. The farmer cut the corn with his sickle. Harvest time had arrived. The farmer's family were happy people. They knew that they would have enough food for the coming year.

Jesus said that God's Kingdom was just like the corn. People hear about Jesus and some believe. They are like the seed in the ground. Nobody knows why some people believe in God and others do not. God alone can answer that question.

DISCUSSION POINTS

1 *Use factsheet 14 to talk about farming in the first century.* Explain the process of producing enough food for a family to eat.

2 *The mysteries of nature.* Do you understand all that goes on around you and on which you depend? Why is the mysterious element important? Draw parallels between those elements which remain mysterious and the growth of God's Kingdom.

The seed

Read Mark 4.26-29.

This is how a farmer in first-century Palestine might describe his life:

" I am a farmer with a wife and five children to feed. The harvest that I gather in at the end of each year is so important. If we have a bad harvest then it is almost impossible to feed everyone. I prepare my land very carefully. I break up the soil so that the seed will fall into it. There must be no big lumps of earth. I walk up and down the earth throwing my seed left and right. I am always followed by many birds who try to eat my seed. They manage to gobble some of it. I just hope that the wind, the rain and the sun come at the right time to help my seeds grow. Mind you, there is not much that I can do about it if they don't. Nor can I make sure that the seed grows. That happens without my help. You can imagine how I feel when the stalks poke through the soil. I feel even better when I cut down the fully grown corn. That is a wonderful feeling. I can feed my family for another year."

Imagine that you are this farmer. Write, in your book, a story of a farming family in the time of Jesus. Describe how hard everyone works when the seed has to be sown.

What kind of things do the family do while the seed is growing in the earth?
How excited is everyone when the first stalks appear?
Do the children go out every day to see how the corn is growing?
What happens when it is time to cut the corn down?
Is everyone happy when the harvest is gathered in?

The talents

AIMS

The aims of this section are to introduce:

1 The Kingdom of God (heaven) which Jesus came to bring

2 The different responsibilities given to the three servants

3 The return of the master.

KEY WORDS

Kingdom of God

Parable

Matthew 25.14-30

1 Servants in the ancient world were often given considerable authority. The man in this parable gives each of his servants varying, but considerable, sums of money to invest while he is away. A 'talent' was a unit of exchange but opinions vary considerably on its value. It probably refers to a sum which would take a working man some fifteen years to earn (so the sums referred to in this story are vast). The number of talents are distributed on the basis of the master's estimates of the servants abilities.

2 Two of the servants went to work 'at once' to increase their master's investments. The third, however, dug a hole and buried the money. When the master returned he called each of the servants to account for what they had done. The first servant who received 5,000 talents reported a 100% profit. So, too, did the second servant who had been given 2,000 talents. Both received the commendation of their master and passed into positions of greater responsibility. The third, however, was condemned. He handed back the thousand talents he had been given in the first place.

3 It makes more sense to widen this parable to take on board the modern sense in which the word 'talent' is used. The master in the story is either God or Jesus. If the master is Jesus then the long journey referred to began when he left the earth. Those left behind, and those who follow, are given talents which they are intended to use. At some time in the future the master (Jesus) will return and expect to receive a return on his investment.

THE STORY

The stories of Jesus were not always easy to understand. One day he told a story about a master who was going to take a long journey. He would be away from home for a long time. He had three servants and he called each one to him in turn. He gave the first servant 5,000 talents. That was a huge sum of money. He gave the second servant 2,000 talents and that, too, was a large sum. To the third he gave 1,000 talents. He went away.

A long time later he returned home. He called the first servant and asked what he had done with the money. The servant told his master that he had worked hard and handed over 10,000 talents (twice as much money as his master had given him in the first place). The master was delighted. He was equally pleased when the second servant said that he had turned his 2,000 talents into 4,000 by investing it wisely. He was not pleased, however, with the third servant. The third servant had been so frightened of his master that he had buried his 1,000 talents.

Another important lesson for people to learn is that God has given us all talents (gifts) to use. He will be pleased when we use them properly. Which talents have you been given?

DISCUSSION POINTS

1 *Imagining that you are the master in the story.* Ask children to imagine they are going away for a long time. They call three of their servants together and give them different sums of money. Why are you doing this? What do you expect them to do with your money? What do you hope to receive when you return?

2 *Ask children to imagine that they are the servant who has been given 1,000 talents.* What are you going to do with it? Why? Do you think that your master will be pleased with what you have done?

 NAME...

The three servants

Read Matthew 25.14-25.

First servant

How much was he given?

What did he do with his money?

Was his master pleased?

Second servant

How much was he given?

What did he do with the money?

Was his master pleased?

Third servant

How much was he given?

What did he do with the money?

Was his master pleased?

Important events in the four Gospels

The birth of Jesus	Matthew 1.18-25; Luke 1.26-2.20
John the Baptist	Matthew 3.1-12; Mark 1.1-8; Luke 3.1-20
Baptism of Jesus	Matthew 3.13-17; Mark 1.9-11; Luke 3.21,22
Temptations of Jesus	Matthew 4.1-11; Mark 1.12,13; Luke 4.1-13
Jesus chooses twelve disciples	Matthew 10.2-4; Mark 3.13-19; Luke 6.12-16
The Sermon on the Mount	Matthew 5-7
Jesus feeds a large crowd	Matthew 14.13-21; 15.29-39; Mark 6.30-44; Mark 8.1-13; Luke 9.10-17; John 6.1-15
Peter's confession	Matthew 16.13-20; Mark 8.27-30; Luke 9.18-27
The Transfiguration	Matthew 17.1-13; Mark 9.2-13; Luke 9.26-36
The Good Samaritan	Luke 10.30-37
Jesus enters Jerusalem	Matthew 21.1-11; Mark 11.1-11; Luke 19.29-40; John 12.12-16
The Last Supper	Matthew 26.17-30; Mark 14.12-26; Luke 22.7-38
The Garden of Gethsemane	Matthew 26.36-46; Mark 14.32-42; Luke 22.39-46
Arrest of Jesus	Matthew 26.47-56; Mark 14.43-52; Luke 22.47-53; John 18.1-11
Denial of Peter	Matthew 26.69-75; Mark 14.66-72;Luke 22.54-62; John 18.15-18,25-27
Jesus before Pilate	Matthew 27.11-26; Mark 15.1-15; Luke 23.1-25; John 18.28-19.16
The crucifixion	Matthew 27.32-44; Mark 15.21-32; Luke 23.26-43; John 19.17-27
The death of Jesus	Matthew 27.45-53; Mark 15.33-41;Luke 23.44-49; John 19.28-37
The burial of Jesus	Matthew 27.57-66; Mark 15.42-47;Luke 23.50-56; John 19.38-42
The resurrection	Matthew 28.1-10; Mark 16.1-8; Luke 24.1-12; John 20.1-31

The teachings of Jesus

As well as narrating the main events in the life of Jesus, the four Gospels include the most important things that he said. The Gospels record the teachings of Jesus about the nature of God and about his own status as Messiah, about prayer, moral issues and much more. Often Jesus taught the people by telling them parables (stories which contain hidden meanings).

A summary of the most important teachings of Jesus is found in the Sermon on the Mount (Matthew 5-7). It is a collection of the key teachings of Jesus about many topics, including:

- the people who will receive God's blessing (5.1-12)
- the Law (5.17-20)
- anger (5.21-26)
- lust and adultery (5.27-30)
- divorce (5.31-32)
- retaliation and loving one's enemies (5.38-48)
- giving to those in need (6.1-4)
- prayer (6.5-14)
- money (6.19-24)
- worrying (6.25-34)
- criticising others (7.1-6).

Some of the material that Matthew groups together in the Sermon on the Mount appears in similar form in Luke 6.20-49. This shorter collection of teachings is sometimes referred to as the Sermon on the Plain.

UNIT FIVE

The parables

The first recorded words of Jesus, found in Mark's Gospel, are, "The right time has come and the Kingdom of God is near." (Mark 1.15). The theme of the Kingdom of God, or the Kingdom of heaven, as it is often called, dominated the teaching of Jesus. It referred to God's rule or reign as King and to the spiritual sphere over which God rules. Nearly all the teaching of Jesus about God's Kingdom was given in the form of parables.

The Jewish rabbis of the time often taught the people through parables. The parables were stories which contained a meaning or message over and above the obvious meaning of the story. Often this message took the form of an extended simile (as when Jesus often said 'The Kingdom of heaven is like...').

There are no parables in John's Gospel. However, the Synoptic Gospels record around 40 different parables told by Jesus.

Parable	Matthew	Mark	Luke
The lamp under a bowl	5.14,15	4.21,22	8.16;11.33
The two house builders	7.24-27	6.47-49	
Cloth and wineskins	9.16,17	2.21,22	5.36-38
The sower and the soils	13.3-9; 18-23	4.3-9;13-20	8.5-8;11-15
The weeds	13.24-30; 36-43		
The mustard seed	13.31,32	4.30-32	13.18,19
The yeast	13.33		13.20,21
The hidden treasure	13.44		
The pearl	13.45,46		
The net	13.47-50		
The lost sheep	18.12-14		15.4-7
The unforgiving servant	18.21-34		
The workers in the vineyard	20.1-16		
The two sons	21.28-32		
The tenants in the vineyard	21.33-44	12.1-11	20.9-18
The feast	22.2-14		14.16-24
The two servants	24.45-51		12.42-48
The ten young women	25.1-13		
The three servants	25.14-30		19.12-27
The sheep and the goats	25.31-46		
The growing seed			4.26-29
The watchful servants	13.35-37	12.35-40	
The money and the money-lender		7.41-43	
The Good Samaritan			10.30-37
The friend in need			11.5-8
The rich fool			12.16-21
The unfruitful fig-tree			13.6-9
The tower and the king			14.28-33
The lost coin			15.8-10
The lost son			15.11-32
The shrewd manager			16.1-8
The rich man and Lazarus			16.19-31
The widow and the judge			18.2-8
The Pharisee and the tax-collector		18.10-14	

UNIT FIVE

The miracles

The writers of the four Gospels believed that God could, and did, intervene in the course of nature and in the lives of individuals. The word 'miracle' came from the Greek word meaning 'wonder' and referred to an event which caused people to stop and wonder. A miracle was an act of supernatural power, and people were aware that Jesus could only perform his miracles through the power of God. In John's Gospel, the miracles were called 'signs', since they signalled God's power to the people. The miracles recorded in the Gospels each fall into one of three categories:

1. *Those which demonstrate the power of Jesus over the forces of nature.* Three miracles demonstrate this most clearly: Jesus calming the storm on the sea of Galilee; Jesus feeding the hungry people; Jesus walking on the water.

2. *Those which show the power of Jesus over the evil spirits which caused distress, illness and suffering to people.* Sometimes he demanded faith from those being cured but, on other occasions, he performed a miracle without the person even being present. Throughout his ministry Jesus is presented as being in a continual battle with the forces of evil and darkness.

3. *Those in which Jesus brought the dead back to life.* This happened on three occasions: the raising of Lazarus's daughter; the raising of the widow of Nain's son; the bringing of Lazarus back to life.

Jesus and nature

	Matthew	Mark	Luke	John
Calming the storm	8.23-27	4.35-41	8.22-25	
Walking on the water	14.22-33	6.45-52		6.16-21
Feeding 5,000 people	14.13-21	6.30-44	9.10-17	6.1-15
Feeding 4,000 people	5.32-38	8.1-9		
Coin in the fish's mouth	17.24-27			
Fig-tree withers	21.18-22	11.12-14	20-24	
Catch of fish				5.1-11
Water into wine				2.1-11
Catch of fish				21.1-11

Healing miracles

	Matthew	Mark	Luke	John
Man with leprosy	8.1-4	1.40-45	5.12-16	
Roman soldier's servant	8.5-13		7.1-10	
Peter's mother-in-law	8.14-17	1.29-34	4.38-41	
Two men from Gadara	8.28-34	5.1-20	8.26-39	
Paralysed man	9.1-7	2.1-12	5.17-26	
Woman with bleeding	9.20-22	5.25-29	8.43-48	
Two blind men	9.27-31			
Mute, possessed man	9.32-34			
Man with paralysed hand	12.9-14	3.1-6	6.6-11	
Blind and mute man	12.23	11.14,15		
Canaanite woman's daughter	15.21-28	7.24-30		
Boy with demon	7.14-21	9.14-29	9.37-43	
Two blind men	20.29-34	10.46-52	18.35-43	
Deaf mute	7.31-37			
Man possessed	1.21-28	4.31-37		
Blind man at Bethsaida	8.22-26			
Crippled woman				3.10-17
Man with swollen limbs				14.1-6
Ten men with leprosy				17.11-19
High Priest's servant			22.49-51	
Official's son				4.43-54
Sick man				5.1-18
Man born blind				9.1-12

Returning the dead to life

	Matthew	Mark	Luke	John
The daughter of Jairus	9.18-19,23-26	5.21-24,35-43	8.40-42,49-56	
The widow of Nain's son			7.11-17	
Lazarus				11.1-44

UNIT FIVE

The last week in the life of Jesus

All of the Gospels are dominated by the events of the last few days in the life of Jesus. The story of the week leading up to his death and resurrection occupies some 30 per cent of Mark's Gospel and only slightly less in the other three. The events of this week, called 'Holy Week', are re-enacted by the Christian Churches in their services each year leading up to Easter.

You will find a map of Jerusalem, where all the events of the last week took place, on page 00.0

Sunday

Matthew 21.1-11; Mark 11.1-11; Luke 19.28-40; John 12.12-19

Crowds waved branches and shouted, "God bless him who comes in the Lord's name". They greeted Jesus as he arrived in the city of Jerusalem. He rode on a donkey fulfilling the words of the Old Testament prophet, Zechariah.

Monday

Matthew 21.12-13; Mark 11.15-17; Luke 19.45-46

Angry that the Temple courts were filled not with people worshipping God but with money-changers and merchants, Jesus drove out the merchants and overturned their tables. He quoted the prophets Isaiah and Jeremiah, saying that God's house should be a house of prayer but it has instead become a hideout for thieves.

Tuesday

Matthew 26.14-16; Mark 14.10,11; Luke 22.3-6

Judas, one of the twelve disciples, approached the chief priests and offered to help them arrest Jesus at a suitable time and place. They eagerly accepted his offer and promised him money (thirty pieces of silver).

Thursday

Matthew 26.30-56; Mark 14.22-50; Luke 22.14-53; John 18.1-11

Jesus shared the traditional Passover meal with his disciples, during which he instructed them to eat bread and to drink wine. He said, "This is my body and my blood". During the meal, Jesus also predicted that Judas Iscariot would betray him, and that Peter would deny him three times.

When the meal was over, Jesus went to the Garden of Gethsemane (an olive orchard on the Mount of Olives) to pray. Jesus asked three of his disciples to pray with him during the night, but they fell asleep more than once. After this, Judas led the Temple guard to Jesus. Judas identified Jesus by kissing him. Jesus did not resist arrest but asked that his disciples be allowed to go free.

Friday

Matthew 26.57-27.56; Mark 14.53-15.41; Luke 22.54-23.49; John 18.13-19.30

In the early hours of Friday, Jesus was brought before the teachers of the Law and the elders to be tried. While he waited outside, Peter was accused three times of being a disciple of Jesus and each time he denied it. Jesus was later brought before Pontius Pilate, the Roman Governor, who condemned him to be flogged, and later crucified.

Jesus was led out to Golgotha (meaning 'the place of the skull') where he was crucified along with two thieves. Between noon and three o'clock, the sky was darkened. At three o'clock, Jesus gave a loud cry and died. That evening, before the Sabbath day began, his body was taken down and buried by a rich Jew, Joseph of Arithmathea, in his own tomb. The tomb was sealed and Roman guards were placed outside.

Sunday

Matthew 28.1-10; Mark 16.1-10; Luke 24.1-12; John 20.1-18

Early on Sunday morning, some women followers of Jesus went to the tomb, hoping to anoint the body. They found the stone rolled away and the tomb empty. Men in shining clothes told them that Jesus had returned to life. Jesus himself later appeared to many of his followers.

UNIT FIVE

The resurrection appearances of Jesus

Event	Date	Matthew	Mark	Luke	John
The empty tomb	Early Sunday morning	28.1-10	16.1-8	24.1-12	20.1-9
Mary Magdalene	Early Sunday morning at the tomb		16.9-11		20.11-18
Travellers on the road to Emmaus	Sunday midday				24.13-32
Peter in Jerusalem	Sunday			24.34	
Ten disciples	Sunday evening		16.14	24.36-43	20.19-25
Eleven disciples	One week later				20.26-31
Seven disciples fishing by the sea	One day at dawn				21.1-23
Eleven disciples on the mountain	Some time later	28.16-20	16.15-18		
At the ascension on the Mount of Olives	40 days later			24.44-49	

Glossary

Abraham: The father of the Jewish nation. He left Ur of the Chaldees and settled in Canaan. Because of Abraham's willingness to sacrifice his only son, Isaac, God made a covenant (agreement) with him. God promised that blessings would fall on Abraham and his descendants for ever.

Angel: The Greek word for a 'messenger'. It is used in the Gospels to refer to heavenly beings who are sent by God to carry divine messages.

Anglican Church: When the Church of England establishes itself beyond this country it is called the Anglican Church.

Annas: The father of Caiaphas. Caiaphas was the High Priest when Jesus was tried. The High Priest was the chairman of the Sanhedrin.

Aramaic: The language in which Jesus taught. There are one or two traces of Aramaic phrases in the Gospels.

Ascension: The event by which Jesus left the earth at the end of his life. Luke is the only Gospel writer to record the ascension.

Baptism: Means 'to dip'. A Jewish practice whereby converts became members of the faith. Used by John the Baptist and, subsequently, the Christian Church as a rite of initiation.

Barabbas: The thief and murderer who was released by Pontius Pilate, in response to public demand, when Jesus was arrested.

Barmitzvah: The ceremony by which a Jewish boy becomes an adult. The visit of Jesus to Jerusalem at the age of twelve was possibly for his barmitzvah.

Bethlehem: A small town 8 km. south of Jerusalem. It was the place of birth of Jesus.

Blasphemy: Any speech which expresses contempt for God. The charge levelled against Jesus by his opponents.

Breaking of Bread: The term that Free Churches use to describe Holy Communion.

Caiaphas: He was the Jewish High Priest. He was also the son-in-law of Annas. He conducted the first trial of Jesus and demanded that Pilate should pass the death sentence on him.

Capernaum: One of the most frequently mentioned towns in the Gospels. On the north-western shore of Lake Galilee.

Christ: The surname of Jesus. Meaning 'anointed by God'.

Circumcision: The Jewish practice of removing a boy's foreskin on the eighth day after his birth. The practice is to show that the child is a member of the Jewish faith.

Court of the Gentiles: The outer courtyard in the Temple. This was the only area in the Temple that Gentiles were allowed to enter.

Court of the Women: The courtyard in the Temple, beyond the Court of the Gentiles. Both Jewish men and Jewish women were allowed to enter this area.

David: The second king of Israel. He captured Jerusalem. He was also the most loved king of Israel.

Dead Sea: An enclosed area of water, 74 km. (46 miles) long and up to 16 km. (10 miles) wide. It has a very high salt content.

Denarius: A silver coin which bore the image of the Roman Emperor. It was the equivalent of the Greek drachma.

Devil: The Prince of Evil. He appears in the story of the temptations of Jesus. Also called 'Satan'.

Disciple: The word means 'learner' and was the title which, according to the Gospels, was accorded to the twelve men chosen by Jesus to be his closest friends.

Divine Liturgy: The term used in the Orthodox Church for Holy Communion.

Easter Sunday (Easter Day): The day on which Christians celebrate the rising of Jesus from the dead.

Elijah: The most notable of the Jewish prophets of the 9th century BC. Jews expected Elijah to return to earth before the Messiah came.

Elizabeth: Wife of the priest, Zechariah, who after years of infertility gave birth to John the Baptist.

Eucharist: 'Thanksgiving'. The term used by many Christians for the service of Holy Communion.

Exodus: The journey which the Israelites (the Jewish people) took to escape slavery in Egypt. They made their way to the Promised Land of Canaan.

Fasting: The practice of going without food for spiritual reasons. Jesus went without food for forty days and nights before being tempted by the Devil.

Frankincense: Aromatic gum found in South West Arabia and Abyssinia, one of the gifts brought by the Magi (the Wise Men) to Jesus.

Gabriel: The name means 'God's mighty man'. One of the four archangels, the carrier of God's messages to Mary and Joseph.

Galilee: The northern part of Palestine. A small area measuring just 70 km. (45 miles) long.

Gentile: A non-Jew.

Golgotha: An Aramaic word meaning 'the place of a skull'. The site for executions outside the city wall of Jerusalem.

Good Friday: The day on which Christians of all denominations remember the death of Jesus.

Gospels: 'Good News'. The four books in the New Testament written by Matthew, Mark, Luke and John.

Heaven: The home referred to, in the Gospels, of God and his angels. Also believed to be the final destination of true believers.

Herod: Herod the Great. He ruled the Kingdom of Judea with great cruelty from 40 BC to his death. He ordered the massacre of young children in Bethlehem in an attempt to kill Jesus.

Herodians: This was a small party, at the time of Jesus, which was dedicated to supporting Herod the Great.

High Priest: This was the leader of the Jews in the Gospels. He alone was able to enter the holy of holies in the Temple, once a year.

Holy Communion: This is the title which is most frequently applied to the central act of worship in the Christian Church.

Holy Spirit: This is the third Person of the Christian Trinity, with God the Father and God the Son. The Holy Spirit continues the work of Jesus on earth.

Holy Week: This is the seven days from Palm Sunday to Holy Saturday. It is kept by the Christian Church as a time for meditation and reflection.

Israel: This is the name given to tribes which combined to make up the nation of Israel in Old Testament times. The term was later applied to the country in which the tribes lived.

James: The brother of John, one of the disciples of Jesus. Called the 'sons of thunder' because of their quick tempers.

Jeremiah: An Old Testament prophet.

Jericho: One of the oldest cities in the world, 15 km. north-east of the junction of the River Jordan and the Dead Sea.

Jerusalem: The city first captured by King David. It was made the capital of Israel and was the city in which Jesus was crucified.

Jew: A member of the Jewish faith.

John the Baptist: The son of Zechariah and Elizabeth in their old age, and the cousin of Jesus. His preaching prepared the people for the coming of Jesus.

Joseph: The husband of Mary, the father of Jesus.

Joseph of Arithmathea: He was a rich Jewish member of the Jewish Sanhedrin. He laid the body of Jesus in his unused tomb after the crucifixion.

Judaism: The faith and practice of the Jewish people.

Judas Iscariot: The disciple who betrayed Jesus for thirty pieces of silver. He later committed suicide.

Kingdom of God: The rule of God on earth. This is the main burden of the preaching of Jesus.

Kingdom of Heaven: See Kingdom of God.

Last Supper: The last meal that Jesus ate with his disciples before he was arrested. It was the meal on which the service of Holy Communion is based.

Levi: The alternative name for Matthew, author of one Gospel.

Levite: An official who worked in the Temple in Jerusalem.

Lord's Supper: The term favoured by many Christians to describe the service of Holy Communion.

Luke: The physician who travelled with Paul on some of his missionary journeys. He was the writer of one of the Gospels.

Magi: The word means 'wise men'. Tradition has identified the Wise Men who visited Jesus as Magi (astrologers).

Magnificat: The lyrical poem based on the psalms from the Old Testament, which was recited by Mary after an angel announced the birth of Jesus to her. It is used by many Christians in worship.

Mark: He accompanied Paul and Barnabus on their missionary journey, and was the writer of one of the Gospels based on the recollections of Peter.

Mary: She was the mother of Jesus.

Mary Magdalene: She was the leader of a group of women who supported Jesus during his ministry. She had been cured of a serious disease by Jesus.

Mass: This is the term used by Roman Catholics to refer to Holy Communion.

Matthew: One of the disciples of Jesus, Matthew was a tax collector, and the writer of one of the Gospels.

Maundy Thursday: This is the day before Good Friday, on which Christians remember the institution of Holy Communion by Jesus at the Last Supper.

Messiah: The term means 'The Anointed One'. This was the leader who the Jewish people expected to be sent by God to deliver them from all of their enemies. Christians believe that Jesus was the promised Messiah.

Miracle: An extraordinary event which does not have any natural explanation.

Moses: The leader of Israel and the giver of the Law of Israel, he led the Israelites on their Exodus from Egypt.

Myrrh: A resinous gum used in perfume and medicine. It is used for the embalming of corpses. Myrrh was one of the gifts brought, by the Wise Men, to Jesus.

Nazareth: A town in South Galilee, halfway between the Sea of Galilee and the Mediterranean Sea, Nazareth was the residence of Mary, Joseph and Jesus.

New Testament: The twenty seven books which make up the second part of the Christian Bible. The New Testament is concerned with the life of Jesus and that of the early Church.

Old Testament: The thirty nine books which make up the first part of the Christian Bible, the Old Testament also forms the Jewish Bible.

Palestine: The country bounded by the Mediterranean on the west and the Syrian desert on the east, Palestine was originally called Canaan (the Promised Land).

Palm Sunday: The day, at the start of Holy Week, when Christians remember the entry of Jesus into Jerusalem on a donkey.

Parable: Stories told by Jesus in the Gospels. They carry a spiritual message.

Passover: The annual Jewish festival which commemorates the escape of the Israelites from slavery in Egypt (see also Pesach).

Paul: The persecutor of the Early Christian Church, he became a disciple. He also went on many missionary journeys and wrote many letters which are preserved in the New Testament.

Pesach: The Jewish festival of Passover.

Peter: The leading disciple of Jesus, his original name was Simon but Jesus called him Peter (meaning 'the rock').

Pharisee: The term means 'separated one'. The Pharisees were a leading Jewish group in the time of Jesus and were noted for their strict observance of the Jewish Law.

GLOSSARY

Pontius Pilate: The Roman Governor of Judaea (AD 26-36), he condemned Jesus to death. He later fell into disgrace and tradition has it that he committed suicide.

Pope: He is the Bishop of Rome and the chief bishop (of the Roman Catholic Church), believed to be descended from Peter.

Prophet: A person called by God to deliver a special message.

Rabbi: The word means 'my master' or 'my teacher' and was the title given in Jewish law to authorised teachers after their training and examination.

Resurrection: This is the central belief of the Christian faith, that Jesus rose from the dead.

Roman Catholic Church: The community of Christians throughout the world which owes allegiance to the Pope.

Sabbath day: The seventh day, the Jewish day of rest. The commemorated rest of God after his six days of creation.

Samaria: A district in the northern part of Palestine.

Samaritans: Inhabitants of Samaria.

Sanhedrin: The highest Jewish Council, the Sanhedrin was made up of seventy one members, which met under the chairmanship of the High Priest. They were the first group to put Jesus on trial.

Sea of Galilee: Also called the 'Lake of Galilee', the Sea of Galilee was the lake at the northern end of the River Jordan.

Simon of Cyrene: He was the African bystander who was commanded to carry the crossbeam of the cross of Jesus to Golgotha.

Son of David: This was the title given to Jesus as the Jewish Messiah. The belief was that the Messiah would be a descendant of the Old Testament King David.

Son of God: The title given to Jesus.

Stations of the Cross: The series of fourteen paintings or carvings arranged around the walls of a Catholic church, depicting the stages leading up to the crucifixion of Jesus.

Sukkoth: The Jewish feast of Tabernacles, celebrated in the autumn. The name was derived from the temporary booths or shelters in which worshippers spend part of the festival.

Sunday: The Christian holy day which is set aside for worship, to replace the Jewish Sabbath.

Synagogue: The word means 'gathering together'. The Synagogue is the place of learning, study and worship where Jews meet.

Synoptic Gospels: The term means 'seeing together' and refers to the three Gospels (Matthew, Mark and Luke) which have much material in common and which present a similar approach to the life of Jesus.

Tabernacles: The Jewish feast of Sukkoth.

Teachers of the Law: Scribes. Those responsible for teaching the Jewish Law.

Temple: A Jewish place of worship in Jerusalem, first built by Solomon and rebuilt by Herod the Great starting in 19 BC. It was finally destroyed by the Romans in AD 70 and was never rebuilt.

Ten Commandments: The most important part of the Jewish Law, also known as the 'Ten Sayings'.

Torah: The basis of the Jewish faith, these are the books of the Law given by Moses and preserved at the start of the Jewish Scriptures.

Thomas: A disciple of Jesus, Thomas doubted that Jesus had risen from the dead until he was invited to place his hands in the wounds.

Transfiguration: The transfiguration of Christ, celebrated on 6th August, was when he became more spiritual and elevated, changing in appearance.

Zealot: An extreme Jewish nationalist group, dedicated to the expulsion of the Romans from Palestine. Two disciples of Jesus were Zealots.

Zechariah: The father of John the Baptist, Zechariah was a priest in the Temple.